DO WE REALLY KNOW WHAT WORKS?

The Philosophy and Science of Evaluating Social Programs

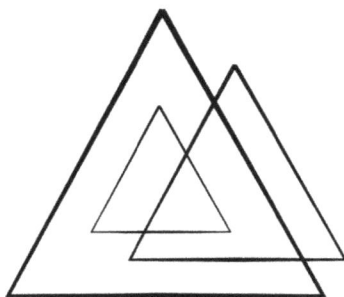

DO WE REALLY KNOW WHAT WORKS?
The Philosophy and Science of
Evaluating Social Programs

ISBN 978-1-938842-68-9

Published by Bardolf & Company
www.bardolfandcompany.com

Cover design by Autumn Kerr of Cultivate Place Creative

To

my wife Elaine

and

our daughter Lisa

who have enriched

my life immeasurably

Also by David E. K. Hunter

Working Hard—and Working WELL

Performance Management and Evaluation
(Ed. with Steffen Bohni Nielsen)

Introduction to Sociology
(with Henry L. Tischler and Phillip Whitten)

The Study of Physical Anthropology and Archaeology
(with Martin K. Nichols and Phillip Whitten)

Readings in Physical Anthropology and Archaeology
(Ed. with Phillip Whitten)

The Study of Cultural Anthropology
(with Phillip Whitten)

The Study of Anthropology
(with Phillip Whitten)

Encyclopedia of Anthropology
(Ed. with Phillip Whitten)

*Doing Anthropology: A Student-Centered Approach
to Cultural Anthropology*
(with MaryAnn B. Foley)

Anthropology: Contemporary Perspectives
(Ed. with Phillip Whitten)

DO WE REALLY KNOW WHAT WORKS?

The Philosophy and Science of Evaluating Social Programs

A meditation for those who use evaluations to design, implement, run, advocate for, and learn from the results of social service programs

David E. K. Hunter

Bardolf & Company
Sarasota, Florida

Contents

Every area of research has...boundaries marking the point at which the process of reflection ceases to be exact and takes on a philosophical character.

—Georg Simmel

Nearly all our knowledge is problematical...and... based on probabilities.

—Pierre Simon, Marquis de Laplace

'Evaluation' has become a mantra of modernity.

—Ray Pawson and Nick Tilley

Most published research findings are false.

—John P. A. Ioannidis

The soundest fact may fail or prevail in the style of its telling.

—Ursula K. Le Guin

PROLOGUE

Depending on one's point of view this oeuvre might be seen as a critical love letter to the evaluation profession or, perhaps more accurately, as what the Germans call a *Streitwerk* or a polite argument with the ways a lot of evaluations of social programs are undertaken. Therefore, I owe the reader some insight into who I am and how my professional career has evolved.

I have had what might be called a meandering professional history. First as a cultural anthropologist, next as a clinical social worker, then as the CEO of a State Psychiatric Hospital, subsequently as director of evaluation at a major foundation, finally as a consultant to public and nonprofit organizations and foundations working in the social sector. And then I retired, only to take on a final job as director of a start-up social investment fund dedicated to improving the lives and prospects of young people who have been cut off from the institutions that should have been nurturing and supporting them. If you are interested, I provide a more detailed narrative in the section "About the Author" at the end of this book.

Why do I mention this here? Well, my travels along this meandering trail have had some consequences. On the upside, each stretch of the road provided me with rich experiences and lots of things I learned, thus informing and enriching my work after the next turn. But there was a downside too. As I entered each turn in my journey I had to immerse myself in the new work quickly, especially where I took on leadership responsibilities. So although I was maturing as a person and developing as a professional through the decades, within each new occupation I was also something of an outsider or at least a beginner with the inevitable insecurities and performance anxieties. This resulted in my adopting, without fully recognizing it, an overdetermined adherence to the prevailing assumptions and beliefs that underlie the work of leaders and practitioners in each new field I entered.

My last few positions brought with them various tasks that involved the evaluation of social programs. And too quickly, as I now see it, I agreed with those in the field who insisted that randomized controlled trials (RCTs) using an experimental design are the "gold standard" of program evaluations when we want to answer the question "Does it work?" as in, for example, The Cornell University Evidence-Based Living blog.[1] In retrospect, for longer than I would have wished, I was rather blinded to conceptual frameworks beyond the one offered by the paradigm grounding much scientific practice in general, and in particular the evaluation of social programs. (This framework, known as positivism, is discussed in Chapter II.) As a consequence, I was underinformed about viable alternative methods for evaluating programs and their results.[2] But time passes and

---

[1] Cornell University Evidence-Based Living blog. "Randomized, Controlled Designs: The "Gold Standard" for Knowing What Works." Accessible at: https://evidence-basedliving.human.cornell.edu/blog/randomized-controlled-designs-the-gold-standard-for-knowing-what-works-2/.

[2] Again in retrospect, while I pretty much understood research methods in the social sciences (about which I had written articles and books), when I first became professionally involved with evaluations of social programs my immediate priority was to develop an understanding of this particular niche—where once again I was an outsider who wanted to join a new community of interest, a stranger in a strange land. At that juncture the priority to learn about this field, its methods, and its practitioners simply crowded out any thoughts of developing a critique of its basic assumptions and beliefs based on issues long explored in the philosophy of science.

I have been working in this area for several decades now, and on occasion even have taken pen to paper to write about it.[3]

Within this context there was an occasion that caused me to begin asking critical questions about RCTs as they are used to evaluate social programs. In 2017 I was part of an advisory group for a multi-site after-school program that was serving young children. In part at my urging, the program's leaders decided to undertake a randomized controlled trial evaluation. The evaluation methodology that ultimately was adopted was far from simple, which in part at least reflected the program's inherent complexity. The study included an implementation evaluation that featured both qualitative and quantitative methods. This was essential for identifying critical implementation issues that then played out in the quantitative research assessing program impacts. These included a large premature dropout rate due to poverty-related family mobility (which meant many children did not receive a full "dosage" of program activities); a high rate of staff turnover; incomplete staff training for late hires; the fact that the program was delivered in school classrooms (and therefore among both staff and participating children, there was an ever-present anxiety about disturbing the teachers' materials and workspace); and a change in leadership at one site.

The consequences of these issues were palpable and led me to wonder whether the quantitative effects that were found (some of them statistically significant) accurately represented the effectiveness of the program model. Or could they be read alternatively as byproducts of implementation turmoil; and in this case, was it really safe to assume the effects would be better if the implementation

---

[3] Hunter, D. E. K. (2013). *Working Hard—and Working WELL*. Hunter Consulting, LLC.

were improved—or is it also possible that this very turmoil unintentionally shielded the children from what might have been less than helpful parts of the program model itself? There was no way to know.

In point of fact, I learned far more from the qualitative part of this evaluation than from the quantitative RCT, something I had not expected. Of course it is now commonplace for evaluators to use both approaches in so-called "mixed method studies," which I discuss in Chapter XIV. But I have come to think that below this superficial mutual hugging there is mischief afoot. What I regard as this false harmony glosses over the profound issue that there are competing and incompatible world views at play here: *instrumentalism* (using quantitative data to make predictions about what new quantitative data will show) and *essentialism* (finding the indispensable characteristics that define the grouping to which something belongs—that is, its essence), both of which are discussed in Chapter V. And as I now see it, *instrumentalism—and particularly positivism in its most rigid form (see Chapter II)—has emerged dominant in our culture.* I believe this is very problematic and discuss this particular concern with some urgency in Chapter XVII, "Applied Epistemology and Why I Wrote This Book."

Here it's also worth mentioning that throughout my adulthood I have been self-consciously aware of a notable gap in my undergraduate and graduate studies—the field of philosophy. Over the years, I read some of the classics; but as an autodidact I didn't know how to traverse this terrain in a focused, methodical manner. And then, rather late in the game, there came yet another meander. In my seventies, I was able to join a reading group of academic philosophers as well as amateur but lifelong students of philosophy. Through our discussions, I began to see threads of thought that I could pull together—ideas that ultimately provided me new and extremely helpful ways to rethink and revise my professional efforts in the domains of performance management and social investing—and especially with regard to the evaluation of social programs.

This book replicates my intellectual journey in highly condensed form. And here I will lay my cards on the table and move rapidly to the most important insight I've gained through these cerebral travels: I have come (belatedly) to understand that, contrary to many public discussions of the matter, there really is no "gold standard" for program evaluations in general—nor for answering the "Does it work?" question. Furthermore, I now see how provisional any findings about program effectiveness and impacts must be regardless of the method(s) used to produce them; how modest we should be in asserting and communicating them; and how tentatively at best we should cling to them.

What follows, though looking closely at the evaluation of social programs, is not a technical discussion of evaluation methods per se. Instead, it is an attempt to explore some of the underlying assumptions that program evaluators make and beliefs they hold—whether tacit or explicit, whether conscious or not—because unless these assumptions and beliefs are understood, those who rely on evaluation findings cannot interpret them confidently (and when they do so, their confidence is hard to justify).

Ultimately, I write this paper with a resolutely utilitarian focus: evaluations of social programs, in my view, are useless unless they can be and are utilized to improve human services so they actually help program participants achieve the results they need to improve their lives and prospects. Why have I bothered? *Because I have an unwavering conviction that when done well and used well program evaluations have a lot to contribute to making the world a better place.*[4]

But as Michael Quinn Patton puts it so well, while the importance of evaluation now is widely accepted, it often is ill used, as manifested in "expecting more than evaluation can deliver, high stakes decision making that goes beyond the evidence, politicalization and distortion of the findings, misuse of evaluations, bloated rhetoric about accountability, huge expenditures on poorly done and useless studies, and a likely decline in quality as demand has outstripped the capacity for high-quality supply."[5]

I have written this book for those who use evaluations to design, implement, run, improve, advocate for, and learn from the results of social programs. I have done so hoping that it will help them approach this work with a deeper understanding of what evaluations can and can't do, what they can and can't mean.

And, of course, I would very much like to know whether I've succeeded. If you are so inclined, your comments can reach me at my email address (*davidekh@outlook.com*).

David E. K. Hunter
Hamden, CT
April 2024

---

[4] Nielsen, S. B. & Hunter, D. E. K. (Eds.) (2013). *Performance Management and Evaluation*. New Directions in Evaluation. 137, Spring.

[5] Patton, M. Q. (2008). *Utilization-Focused Evaluation* (4th edition). Sage. (p. xvii).

INTRODUCTION

Generally speaking, books and papers that discuss program evaluation tend to be narrowly technical or methodological in nature and not about questions such as the age-old problem of how we know what we know and how we come to know it—or, as the philosopher Henry G. Frankfurt puts it, "deciding what to believe"[6]—that is, what philosophers call *epistemology*.

Program evaluations inherently are epistemic undertakings. They're about getting to know things about programs and their effects. Depending on one's framework of inquiry and the assumptions and beliefs that underly it, the questions one asks about a program, and the nature of the data that will be developed and used to answer them will vary considerably. To be sure, there is a literature exploring epistemic issues with regard to program evaluations,[7] some of which I will discuss at various points as their importance becomes pertinent to a topic being explored. However, this literature is exceedingly small in comparison to the literature on evaluation methods. I regard this as a weakness of the evaluation profession, and understand it as one among myriad manifestations of our society's monolithic adoption of a positivist perspective, as will be discussed

---

[6] Frankfurt, H. G. (1998). "The importance of what we care about." *The Importance of What We Care About*, p. 80. Cambridge University Press.

[7] See for example: Guba, E. G. & Lincoln, Y. S. (2005). "Paradigmatic Controversies, Contradictions, and Emerging Confluences." In Denzin, N. K. & Linkoln, Y. S. (eds.) The SAGE Handbook of Qualitative Research. (pp 191-215). SAGE. .

in various ways in Chapter I and throughout what follows. Here I will state a strongly held view that *technical discussions of program evaluation that leave epistemic assumptions and beliefs unexamined can and often do project a spurious aura of exactness regarding what we can learn and know about programs and their results.*

To clarify: this work is best read both as a historical and philosophical essay *and* as a look at evaluation methods themselves. But in the end, my purpose is entirely utilitarian: to help practitioners, the evaluators of their programs, their consultants, their funders, and policymakers better understand and select the research method(s) that in each case will shed at least some light on the questions to which they want answers. And to help them do so in an informed way rather than relying on received wisdom and prevailing fads of thought.

For all of my professional life I have worked as a social scientist and then in the social sector. This frames the range of my relevant knowledge. Therefore, this book is limited to considering the topic of evaluation solely with regard to social programs, although I do believe that many of the issues which I discuss are relevant to the topic of evaluation in other domains as well.

In what follows, I focus on two major contemporary approaches to program evaluations: (a) *randomized controlled trials (RCTs)* because they are widely accepted (at least in the United States) as the "scientific standard" or even the "gold standard" for "proving"[8] whether programs are effective—whether they "work";

---

[8] The widespread belief that the effectiveness of social programs can be "proven" makes program evaluations a high-stakes undertaking and is reflected in the following statement from the website of the Coalition for Evidence-Based Policy: "Programs meeting the highest standards for proven effectiveness should receive top priority for funding, so as to expand them widely and benefit many thousands of people." (emphasis in original) Accessible at: Coalition for Evidence-Based Policy | Tackling US Social Problems Through Evidence About "What Works" (evidencebasedpolicy.org).

and (b) *realist evaluations* because this approach has gained wide currency around the world but remains relatively unknown in the United States. Furthermore, these approaches are rooted in very different schools of epistemic thought; the former in *positivism*, the latter in *realism* (see Chapters VI and IX respectively). So comparing and contrasting them can illuminate fundamental epistemic questions with which evaluators and those who make use of evaluations need to grapple.

But before I dive into a discussion of RCTs and realist evaluations, I find it necessary to draw back a bit in order to provide an historical context. In this way I hope to make what at first may appear to be controversial and maybe even upsetting arguments more palatable and ultimately more plausible. Toward that end, I retrace the history of epistemology as a field of study in itself, with a focus on the most significant differences of opinion that it has produced. I begin with the ancient Greeks and outline (in admittedly limited and simplified ways) the line of evolving thought about such matters in Western Civilization.[9] Along the way we will linger together to reflect, among other things, on the nature of *time and causality* and also on what it means to be objective. This will ease us into an exploration of contemporary epistemic issues that evaluation has

---

[9] I am fully aware that various means of investigating and developing theories about the world around us have origins in civilizations well beyond the borders of Europe—including the Middle East, Southern Asia, China, Africa, and the Americas. However, I am not well enough versed in those endeavors and so I am limiting the scope of this oeuvre to the history of epistemology in the so-called Western world as this pertains to the development and nature of science in general and then, specifically, to the scientific evaluation of social programs. I welcome efforts to broaden my horizons and strengthen the ideas in this work by anyone interested in bringing to this discussion facts about relevant developments in other parts of the world.

yet to address coherently as a discipline. These materials are covered in Chapters I through V.[10]

I hope that despite the obvious limitations of this work it will contribute to a deepening of the reader's appreciation of both the possibilities and limitations of science, the diversity of its epistemic foundations, and the strengths and limitations of its methods—including those of social science and, of course, more specifically of program evaluations. Furthermore, I hope that readers will see value in incorporating evaluation into the day-to-day management of program performance[11]—ultimately to the benefit of those people whom their programs are intended to help.

For now, I beg the reader to be patient. This book is a critical inquiry into the assumptions and beliefs underlying program evaluations. In order for me to achieve this, it is essential that I place program evaluation within the context of scientific thought and practice—it is, after all, an applied (social) science. And to do this meaningfully, I find it essential to look at these matters historically. Accordingly, Chapter I reviews the fundamental debate that for some three hundred years has roiled in the philosophy of science: the struggle between idealism and materialism. Then, Chapter II sketches a history of major questions with which science has had to grapple: first, how to understand the nature of reality; second, what constitutes knowledge and how do (or should) we go about

---

[10] Some readers may be put off that the history covered in this book focuses exclusively on what nowadays are called "white old men." I wish it could have been otherwise. But for an autodidact like me the literature that is most known and available indeed has been written by members of this group. I will leave it to professional historians and philosophers to fill the gap in our knowledge the way it has, over the past three decades or so, been filled in the domains of art and literature where the contributions of women, queer people, and members of diverse ethnic groups have been acknowledged and are a major focus of contemporary study.

[11] Nielsen, S. B. & Hunter, D. E. K. (Eds.) (2013). Op. cit.

creating it; and third, what is objectivity. These questions are, of course, fundamental to the work of evaluating social programs.

For some readers, these two chapters may be somewhat rough sledding. And it is possible, though in my mind not desirable, to bypass them. Nevertheless, for those who do so, I have included a Synopsis of their major points at the end of the book. Having them in mind will provide a meaningful context for the lines of thought discussed in the rest of the book.

A final note regarding the flow of this book. Like my own journey, it will meander at times and even turn back to revisit things that were discussed earlier. Yet each time I will be approaching the point at hand within a somewhat different context and with a different focus or a new emphasis. I hope that such repetitions are helpful and in the end that the whole amounts to more than the aggregate of its parts.

Upon further reflection on what I have written, it strikes me that, appearances aside, the present oeuvre while admittedly a *Streitwerk* is more fundamentally a love letter to evaluation. A fond farewell, if you will. I have entered the ninth decade of my life and, it seems, I am now fully retired. Indeed, as my Swiss friends in Bern would say, *Du wirsch aut. Ja gäu, so geits äbe!*[12]

---

[12] *You're getting old. Ain't it the truth, so it goes!*

Chapter I

EPISTEMOLOGY—THE SEARCH
FOR REALITY IN WESTERN CIVILIZATION

Epistemology is the study of how we learn about the world and to what degree it is reasonable for us to be confident about our discoveries, about what we think we know, and about what we believe is real. Since the beginning of Western philosophy the problem of knowing what "truly" is real (what philosophers call "ontological reality")—versus what we perceive or believe to be real—has proved vexing and resistant to untangling. Even to the present day this issue has not been resolved and shows no promise that it will be in the foreseeable future. Ultimately, the debate is between what generally are referred to as *idealism* and *materialism.* So after considering some relevant philosophical history, we'll take a serious look at these schools of thought and their epistemic premises.

What Our Senses Can
and Can't Tell Us About "Reality"

Broadly speaking philosophy, the "love of wisdom," consists of efforts by dedicated thinkers to comprehend themselves and the world in which they live, and what can be understood about the relationship between humans and whatever is "out there" that is the source of what our senses convey to us.

The Pre-Socratics

In Western Civilization the beginnings of philosophy generally are traced back to fragmentary writings from the sixth century B.C.E. And there we find the origins of a debate that to this day has not been settled. On the one hand, we have the position argued by Parmenides (515 B.C.E.–c. 440 B.C.E.) that nothing can change—that reality is static, that something either exists or it does not. Things can get replaced by new things that once again are static. So, for example, ice is ice, water is water. For him what we think of ice melting, that is, changing into water, is an illusion. On the other hand, we have the perspective of Heraclitus (540 B.C.E.–c. 480 B.C.E.) who saw a world in constant flux where, as is attributed to him, one can never step into the same river twice. What all things have in common is the pattern of change itself.[13]

Of the two, the static view of Parmenides is, intuitively, the harder one to grasp. However, it is far from irrelevant to modern physicists. Albert Einstein refuted the conception of time as absolute and ubiquitous in 1905[14] when he published his Special Theory of Relativity, which showed that time "dilates"—it actually speeds up or slows down for a given entity in relationship to its speed of travel through what now is called space-time, as measured from a separate platform. Consequently, this "does not allow us to constrain existence to merely a moment that we call 'now.' Once

---

[13] Silverman, A. (2022). "Plato's Middle Period Metaphysics and Epistemology." *The Stanford Encyclopedia of Philosophy* (Fall Edition). Zalta, E. N. & Nodelman,, U. (eds.). Accessible at: https://plato.stanford.edu/archives/fall2022/entries/plato-metaphysics/.

[14] Einstein, A. (1905). "Über einen die Erzeugung und Verwandlung des Lichtes betreffenden heuristischen Gesichtspunkt" [On a Heuristic Viewpoint Concerning the Production and Transformation of Light]. *Annalen der Physik*. Vierte Folge (in German). Johann Ambrosius Barth.

you agree that *anything* exists now elsewhere, even though you see it only later, you are forced to accept that *everything* in the universe exists now"[15] (emphasis in the original). Which means that in what has been labeled the block universe, the past, present, and future all coexist statically (even though we experience them changing sequentially).[16]

And what, it would be fair to ask, is the relevance of Parmenides' static view of the world to the evaluation of social programs? In fact, it lies below the surface of randomized controlled trials (RCTs) where the use of statistical methods of analysis communicates an "all or nothing" view of outcomes, a forced bifurcation of what actually is a continuum of change—something discussed more fully in Chapter VIII.

However, the contrasting dynamic perspective of Heraclitus is very compatible with the way we normally think about things. In modern thought it is perhaps best exemplified in the writings of Alfred North Whitehead, who held that reality ultimately is nothing but interrelated processes[17]—as is noted in Chapter VIII. The issue of change and how to understand it will be an ongoing thread throughout the course of this book. And this holds true in the area of program evaluation, where the goal is to discover, document, and understand changes that take place (or, perhaps, fail to do so). Indeed this is a central tenet of so-called "realist evaluations," as will be examined in Chapters IX, X, and XI.

---

[15] Hossenfelder, S. (2022). *Existential Physics: A Scientist's Guide to Life's Biggest Questions*. Atlantic Books. p. 11

[16] As a corollary of the idea of the block universe, individual agency and free will become meaningless, or better said, are seen as a necessary illusion we need to get us through each day and ultimately through our lives in ways that are pragmatically helpful.

[17] Whitehead, A. N. (1933). *Adventures of Ideas*. Simon & Schuster; 1967 edition, The Free Press.

Plato and Aristotle

While Socrates (470–399 B.C.E.) lives on with us through his method of posing questions, nothing remains of his writing. What we know of him we find in the works of his student Plato (c. 429–347 B.C.E.), to whom we turn next.

Plato (c. 429–347 B.C.E.) was skeptical regarding the truthfulness of our perceptions and consequently our knowledge of the world. In his book *The Republic* (375 B.C.E.) he argued famously that we are like figures in a cave who see shadows on the wall and mistake them for what is real, for the entities that actually are behind them but in front of a large fire and consequently are casting those shadows. For him, reality consisted of what he called ideas (that now commonly are referred to as "*forms*"[18]—ideas that are eternal and fixed, such as mathematics. *These "forms" exist beyond the direct reach of human senses and thus, when they are discovered, they are discovered deductively—through reason alone.*

Plato creates a framework for understanding the story of the cave by first using the metaphor of a vertical line divided into two parts with levels within them. Below the divide is the sensible world, the object of mere opinion; above it is the intelligible world discovered through mathematics and pure reason alone and therefore beyond what we can learn through our sense experiences. At the highest level above the divide he places *thought itself*; below thought (but still above the divide) is *how thought has been applied*—namely understanding. Below the divide is how we experience the observable world of animals, plants, and all other material things—or what he thinks of as our *opinions*; and below opinions, he puts *imagination* consisting of what we might say

---

[18] My thanks to the philosopher Melvin Woody for clarifying to me the equivalence of "ideas" and "forms" in Plato.

are indirectly created images such as reflections in mirrors and shadows.[19]

An example might help here. Imagine that we are holding an apple and we state flatly that it is (mostly) red. To us its "redness" is real. But actually, what we are "seeing" is a narrow slice of the spectrum of electromagnetic radiation, the wavelengths that the human eye can register—that is, what we call "light." And within that small range of the spectrum, there is a smaller range that we call "red." But the "redness" of the apple isn't "out there." We have an a priori mental category[20] "red" that we use to slice up the spectrum of light and identify "redness" as we see it. In fact, the world "out there"—in this case the electromagnetic spectrum, is colorless. Plato would say that the color red is an idea, a form. As are all colors. We use that idea to organize the world around us into a palette of colors to understand the world (we can tell the difference between our "red" apple and a "green" Granny Smith apple). And we form opinions about the world using our understanding. In this example, what we experience as the "redness" of the apple is an opinion we hold, is subjective, ephemeral, and ultimately not to be trusted: it isn't knowledge. In contrast, the idea of "redness" is what endures and thus is part of our knowledge.[21]

Aristotle (384–322 B.C.E.), a student of Plato's, systematized this way of thinking by postulating *categories of existence*, some of which are discovered deductively through reasoning alone (like

---

[19] Plato. (375 B.C.E./2006). (Allen, R. E. translator and editor) *The Republic*. Yale University Press. pp. 223-227.

[20] A priori categories are arrived at solely through logical deduction or taught to us, not through the analysis of observed or measured things or events.

[21] The fact that the particular colors we recognize are to a significant degree specific to each culture doesn't undercut this example: for each of us in our respective cultures, the colors we see are a priori categories.

Plato's *forms*) and are constant and hence universal; but he also recognized that there are real things in the world that are accessible to our senses. He emphasized, however, that their reality is subjective, particular to each person's perception of them, and that they are fleeting and constantly changing through time (rivers flow, mountains erode, people age—and social programs are shifted or drift in their implementation). Philosophers through the ages have tended to adopt Aristotle's way of thinking—that is, categorically separating what we can experience via our senses from the external "reality" beyond human experience—and ceded to a very small number of highly intelligent, sensitive, and thoughtful individuals the ability to see behind what we can experience through our senses and who, through reasoning alone, have the ability to propose the characteristics of unchanging universals. That is, of "reality."

Although there has been some tweaking of this perspective across the subsequent two millennia, the prevailing approach has changed little—in no small part due to the hegemony of Christianity as the dominant and determinative worldview of European society. The paradigm remained: that the perceived world is transient and incomplete, whereas the search for truth or reality should be the pursuit of what is constant about the universe—for example, so-called "natural laws" that are presumed to be true at all times everywhere, such as Isaac Newton's laws of gravity and motion. And, of course, the divinity. So let's jump ahead to the 1600s.

Continental Rationalism—Descartes and Spinoza

The 1600s were a time of turmoil and rapid change in Europe. The Thirty Years War (1618–1648) and the English Civil War (1642–1649) tore apart previous social, political and even religious institutions. Inevitably philosophical thinkers broke new ground as they explored what it means to be a rational human being.

The expression "continental rationalism" refers to a set of views more or less shared by a number of philosophers active on the European continent during the latter two-thirds of the 17th century and the beginning of the 18th. To be a rationalist requires at least one of the following: (1) a privileging of reason and intuition over sensation and experience, (2) regarding all or most ideas as innate rather than adventitious, and (3) an emphasis on certain rather than merely probable knowledge as the goal of inquiry.[22]

Generally speaking, this development is seen as creating the foundation for modern science.

The French philosopher Rene Descartes (1596–1650) saw reality as divided into two realms: the material world of things that have spacial extension, including the human body (and hence the brain); and those things having no extension in the material world, especially the world of the spirit or mind (which he believed to be a manifestation of the divinity in each person). Based on this dualist perspective, Descartes took skepticism about what can be known to the extreme when he pronounced his famous credo *Cogito ergo sum* ("I think therefore I am"). He trusted his understanding of reality only to the degree that he could reason about what his senses told him and then reflect inwardly on the processes of his thinking. In this way, he could develop "true" ideas about reality. Worth noting is that he is thought to be the "father" of modern philosophy, specifically *rationalism*. Rationalists value intuition and reasoning over experiences gained through the senses, pursue the achievement of

---

[22] Shannon, D., Walsch, J. & Lennon, T. M. (2018). "Continental Rationalism." *The Stanford Encyclopedia of Philosophy* (Winter Edition), Edward N. Zalta (ed.). Accessible at: https://plato.stanford.edu/archives/win2018/entries/continental-rationalism/.

certainty (which our senses can never establish for us), and think of ideas as generated internally via deduction rather than discovered inductively through analysis of what our senses convey to us.

Born in Amsterdam to a Portuguese-Jewish family, the philosopher Baruch Spinoza (1632–1677) was in some ways even more of a radical skeptic than Descartes. He rejected the conventional notion of an infinite god, the divine origin of the Bible, the attributed authorship of the Pentateuch and various other biblical books, and the authority of both Jewish and Christian religious institutions (which he dismissed as cults)—for which he ultimately was excommunicated from the Jewish community at the age of 24. To this day he is esteemed as a courageous thinker in a time of chaos. While he shared and built on Descartes' rationalism, he differed from Descartes in his monist view that all existence is material or, like the mind, is grounded in the material (the brain)[23]. Thus he contributed mightily to the intellectual foundation from which modern science emerged—including, with regard to the concerns of this book, the social sciences.

Philosophy With a Focus on Cause and Effect

It was, however, Descartes's radical rationalism that proved to be an inflection point for European philosophy. It became the dominant paradigm of Western thought for several hundred years and was taken to the extreme by David Hume (1711–1776), a giant of Western philosophy who championed an uncompromising idealism.[24] In his *Enquiries Concerning Human Understanding* (1748)

---

[23] Spinoza, B. d. (1670). *Theological-Political Treatise*. Israel, J. (editor) Cambridge University Press.

[24] Morris, W. E. and Brown, C. R. (2023) "David Hume." *The Stanford Encyclopedia of Philosophy* (Winter Edition). Zalta, E. N. & Nodelman, U. (eds.). Accessible at: https://plato.stanford.edu/archives/win2023/entries/hume/.

and other works, Hume argued that trying to know "what is out there" is a hopeless undertaking. Indeed, for Hume, the world "out there" really doesn't have any meaning unless and until a human mind has discerned it by sorting sense perceptions into pre-existing or a priori mental categories (that is the categories of time and space). In this manner *we build or create what is "real," what is "out there," for pragmatic human purposes*—but keep the ultimate nature of "reality" securely confined to the workings of the mind. His argument disturbed many traditional (and particularly religious) thinkers who derided him as a "skeptic" and, even worse, castigated him as an atheist since he relegated all theological thinking to the realm of metaphysics—i.e., the world of the unprovable.[25] Yet Hume influenced many of the most advanced thinkers of his day, including Jeremy Bentham, Adam Smith, and Charles Darwin.[26]

Hume's skepticism, including his *rejection of the notion of causality* (which he dismissed as metaphysical speculation), has never been refuted credibly, although alternatives have been proffered—most notably by another giant of Western philosophy, Immanuel Kant (1724–1804). Kant credits Hume for having shocked him awake

---

[25] In this view theology made no sense at all, was indeed an inherently irrational undertaking that lacks any means to test or validate its pronouncements. One theologian's opinions are just as (in)valid as any other's—except, of course, when a plenum of an ecumenical council votes on which "truth" to validate in the name of god. As indeed the first ecumenical counsel did when it met in Constantinople in 381 C.E. and adopted the so-called Trinitarian Doctrine that held the Father, the Son, and the Holy Spirit to be equal. However, lest we be too quick to deride this questionable way of establishing truth, we should remember that the American Psychiatric Association's board of trustees in 1973, with a metaphorical flick of the wrist but with no new evidence to guide them, by a simple vote declared that homosexuality, which they had previously defined as a mental disorder, is not pathological at all. For which we can all be thankful. Belatedly.

[26] Hume's work also underlies some of the frontiers of contemporary research, notably studies in cognitive neuroscience. See, for example, the dialogue between the philosopher Paul Ricoeur and the neuroscientist Jean-Pearre Changeux: Changeux, J.-P. & Ricoeur, P. (2000). *What Makes us Think?* Princeton University Press.

from his "dogmatic slumber" (that is, his conventional habits of thought), but he could not accept Hume's pure and rigid idealism lock, stock, and barrel. He criticized Hume's rejection of causality due to its metaphysical nature; instead, Kant insisted that causality is a valid scientific idea, arrived at through rigorous deductive reasoning that then is tested materially via formal experimentation or other empirical experiences.

In his *Critique of Pure Reason* (1781), Kant believed that he had rescued causality in two steps. First, he stipulated that cause and effect are pure, deductively discovered *a priori* concepts that are created in and by the mind without reference to any input from the senses. So far this is pure Hume. But then Kant went on to the second step, arguing that causality, though *a priori* in its categorical nature, in its application is limited in terms of its contents to what our senses, our experiences reveal to us. As Kant put it, the concepts of cause and effect only can exist "in the relation of the understanding to experience, however, not in such a way that they are derived from experience, but that experience is derived from them, a completely reversed kind of connection which never occurred to Hume."[27] The 18th-century poet and philosopher Friedrich Schiller, a follower of Kant, observed that we are "tempted to model the real after the intelligible, and to raise the subjective laws of [our] imagination into laws constituting the existence of things"[28]—that is, to elevate the "laws" of our intellect into "laws of nature." This, he argued, is a mistake. And, as will become evident later, this also

---

[27] Quoted in De Pierris, G. & Friedman, M. (2018). "Kant and Hume on Causality." The Stanford Encyclopedia of Philosophy (Winter Edition). Edward N. Zalta (ed.), URL = <https://plato.stanford.edu/archives/win2018/entries/kant-hume-causality/>.

[28] Schiller, F. (2015). Originally published in 1795. *Letters on the Aesthetical Education of Man*. Grindel Press. p. 31.

characterizes some of the problematic ways in which some program evaluators approach their work (see Chapters II and IV).

To be clear: Kant believed in a physical world where things exist regardless of whether they are observed or experienced by human beings. He uses the term *Ding an sich* ("thing in and of itself") to refer to that "external" world. In this sense, he brought a gentle kind of materialism into his thinking. However, he insisted that only when we analyze our sensory inputs emanating from our encounters with things in this "external" world, when we fit them into mental a priori categories, that we then have what we call *sensory representations* or experiences of this world. In other words, our experiences of this world are mind-dependent (that is, "subjective"); but the substance, the material of the world is not mind-dependent. It exists independently of us (thus it is "objective").[29] But the objective world only can be approached. It can't ever be known fully.

Kant's paradigm became the basis for at least another hundred years of philosophical inquiries and scientific research; there was widespread acceptance of his formulation that *reality as we know it is inwardly constructed or "subjective"* (although it is constrained by what our senses tell us)—as opposed to "objective" reality that is somehow "out there." But there also was recognition that any understanding of subjective "reality" has the potential to be amended (or even jettisoned) as methods of scientific inquiry develop. For this reason, we might think of Kant as what could be called a "soft" idealist. It also leads us to the kind of thinking on which we rely when we evaluate social programs.

---

[29] Stang, N. F. (2023). "Kant's Transcendental Idealism." *The Stanford Encyclopedia of Philosophy* (Winter Edition). Accessible at: https://plato.stanford.edu/archives/spr2024/entries/kant-transcendental-idealism/.

The Two Basic Versions of Idealism

Idealism has two basic versions. In the first, commonly viewed as the stronger version, all reality is considered to be a product of the mind; it is referred to as "metaphysical idealism" or "ontological idealism." As we have seen, in this view reality ultimately consists of our internal mental structures (the categories in terms of which we make sense of the world); these organize our thoughts and are the basis for how we give meaning to sensory inputs and thereby create perceptions—perceptions of what for us is the "real world." It is these mental categories that modern idealist philosophers and scientists look at in order to think about and thereby understand the world. Their work is *deductive*, consisting of the *logical analysis of ideas about what is real.* Looking at programs and their evaluation through this lens entails research methods to study what can be observed about a program, its activities, and subsequent developments with regard to its participants. This is followed by a logical analysis using predetermined constructs (e.g., quantitative means to determine statistical significance) to draw conclusions about cause and effect, that is, about the program and its outcomes.

The second version of idealism is grounded in Kant's work and acknowledges that there are important things which exist and endure and are independent of the human mind. Nevertheless, it holds to the view that "everything that we can know about this mind-independent 'reality' is...so permeated by the creative, formative, or constructive activities of the mind...that *all claims to knowledge must be considered, in some sense, to be a form of self-knowledge*"[30] (emphasis

---

[30] Guyer, P. & Horstmann, R.-P. (2023). "Idealism", *The Stanford Encyclopedia of Philosophy* (Spring Edition). Edward N. Zalta & Uri Nodelman (eds.). Accessible at: https://plato.stanford.edu/archives/spr2023/entries/idealism/.

added). This version often is termed "formal" or "epistemological idealism." And it will prove to be very important in the discussion of what are called "realist" program evaluations. As we shall see in Chapter IX, realist evaluation considers programs to be theories whose hypotheses are to be tested and revised iteratively.

Here then, we see an idealism that is suitable as a perspective in terms of which to investigate programs and their effects. However, it also makes clear that we should do so only very tentatively and only with constant evaluative review.

Materialism Emerges and Challenges Idealism

In the 17th century with the emergence of the industrial revolution, the gauntlet was thrown down and idealism was challenged full bore. In what amounted to an assault, this challenge marched to the banner of *materialism*, the general idea of which is that the nature of the universe and everything in it is physical, is material—or at least can ultimately be explained by physical facts.[31] And today, science still is commonly understood to be a particular kind of materialism—a very intentional, rigorous, systematic approach to learning about the observable world—the observable world that includes human beings in general and, therefore, social programs too.

Materialism is grounded in observation and measurement and depends principally on induction, the analysis of accumulated experiences (rather than the analysis of ideas about experiences). Induction consists of putting things that have been observed and measured into aggregated categories, some of which are the product of past efforts and others of which are developed de novo using

---

[31] For this reason, materialism in many quarters is seen as a full frontal attack on religion. A view that is not, however, shared by all scientists nor even all theologians. For example, see the theoretical physicist Sabine Hossenfelder's engaging book on what she calls "existential physics": Hossenfelder, S. (2022). Op. cit.

the new data. In both cases of categorization, this involves stripping out of consideration any unique qualities of the entities being analyzed that would prevent them from being grouped together. So it is essential to bear in mind that all categorization—inductive or deductive—inherently involves simplification. Thus scientific analysis, too, inherently amounts to simplification. This is a caveat that is very relevant to program evaluations and the claims that are made about what they can and can't discover, what they can and can't prove.

While it is tempting to think of modern science as inherently materialist, this is too crude a view, and in some domains idealist thinking in the sciences is pronounced.[32] The fact that both materialism and idealism continue to influence science is relevant to program evaluations since they operate within the domain of applied social science the way mechanical engineering is an applied form of physics. So to understand program evaluation as an applied science we really should understand science itself—or at least those aspects of science that pertain to the theory and methods of program evaluations. But this begs the question: "What is science?" To answer that question, it seems to me, that we first should answer a more basic one: "How did science come into being?"

These questions are explored in the following chapter. And along the way, we should wonder why, in the United States, when the matter at hand is establishing programs' results, evaluations

---

[32] For example in the realm of cosmology where, at least until recently, our understanding of the universe relied on the view that about 95 percent of it consists of an inherently unobservable combination of black matter and black energy whose presence was inferred by manifestations of cosmological behavior that we could not otherwise explain (the expansion of the universe and the spinning of galaxies); and this perspective produced the leading assumption long shared among cosmologists, that our universe began with a "big bang"—which now is a highly questionable belief given recent data provided by the James Webb Space Telescope.

mostly rely on methods that reflect the most reductive kind of materialism. This approach, called positivism, will be explored in the chapters that follow, culminating in Chapter VI.

Chapter II

A BRIEF HISTORY OF WESTERN SCIENCE

Western science emerged from the world of philosophy. Seeds for its development can already be found in the fourth century B.C.E. in the thought of Plato and Aristotle, both of whom emphasized the importance of observing nature rigorously. In his *Organon,*[33] Aristotle discussed the two major forms of reasoning that remain to this day fundamental to science: *inductive reasoning through generalization from discovered facts*, and *deductive reasoning involving the logical analysis of such generalizations to discover their implications.*

A full millennium and a half later in the Middle Ages, various scholars including Thomas Aquinas (1224/25–1274) operationalized the differences between induction and deduction by establishing what could and could not reasonably be discovered inductively from our accumulated sensory experiences.[34] This line of thinking was clarified by Roger Bacon (c. 1219–c. 1292), who argued explicitly that inductive "experimental methods alone give certainty in science."[35]

---

[33] Although Aristotle lived and taught in the 4th century B.C.E., his works were not collected and published until two centuries later in 50 B.C.E.

[34] Hepburn B. and Anderson H. (2021). "Scientific Method." *The Stanford Encyclopedia of Philosophy*. (Summer Edition), Edward N. Zalta (ed.), URL = <https://plato.stanford.edu/archives/sum2021/entries/scientific-method/>.

[35] Dampier, W. C. (1929). *A History of Science and its Relations with Philosophy and Religion*. Cambridge University Press. p. 90.

But it was not until the emergence and flourishing of the so-called Enlightenment, spanning the 16th through the 18th centuries, that received wisdom lost its iron grip on human thought. Questioning virtually everything became the Western leitmotif, in no small part inspired by the Protestant Reformation of the 16th century when the range of what could be thought about, written about, and debated openly was extended into new domains and was laying the intellectual foundation for radical economic and political change.[36] It was a time of profound shifts across all aspects of society, including a redefinition of the rights of kings in England and the beginnings of what eventually became parliamentary rule. Isaac Newton and Gottfried Leibnitz were independently "inventing" calculus, Shakespeare was inventing psychology, Rembrandt was laying the groundwork for impressionism,[37] Mozart was stretching musical forms to their extremes, and Galileo was dropping things from the Tower of Pisa to study gravity. It was a time when the Industrial Revolution was shifting production out of the household and into factories while moving rural populations out of agrarian society into cities. In all senses of the word, it was a time of revolutions.

Amid all this turmoil a lawyer and eventual High Chancellor of England named Francis Bacon (1561-1626) articulated the first

---

[36] Weber, M. (1958) Originally published in 1905. *The Protestant Ethic and The Spirit of Capitalism*. Scribners.

[37] The emergence of impressionism generally is located in the 19th century as manifested in the work of Claude Monet, Camille Pissarro, Marie Cassatt and other painters. However, a hundred years earlier Rembrandt had broken loose from the practice of outlining objects and often was painting only with small brushstrokes of color, which is among the hallmarks of the impressionist school. I want to make this point because it is easy to overinvest in the recent or contemporary and forget that we all stand on the shoulders of others. Similarly, Archimedes of Syracuse (287-212 B.C.E.) laid the foundation for calculus when he discovered the value of "pi"—but conventional history tells us that calculus was in "invented" some 2,000 years later by Leibnitz and Newton.

formal theory of science in his *Novum Organum* (1620)[38]. In it he proposed that science requires objectivity—the collection of data without preconceptions and the gradual building of knowledge through constant adjustments in thinking as new facts emerge. Indeed, he believed such objective research ultimately would yield explanations for the causes of things in the form of general laws of nature.[39] And this formulation became the foundation of the scientific revolution.

But what is objectivity?

Objectivity: the Bedrock of Modern Western Epistemology

Today, we take reliance on objectivity for granted and value it highly in many contexts—including the evaluation of social programs and their impacts. But for several thousand years in Western civilization, the concept of objectivity itself had little or no meaning whatsoever. Not for Plato nor Aristotle, not for Descartes, not for Hume nor Kant. Western philosophers simply didn't think about the matter of objectivity, in part because they were concerned with subjects like eternal ideas or forms to be intuited, or on theological postulates that focused on ontological issues (the nature of existence in general) and the exploration (through reasoning) of universal constants or things that never change—i.e., what they called the laws of nature. In these spheres, the question about whether the thinker is being objective simply does not arise. It is enough that she or he is engaging in disciplined, well-reasoned, and well-communicated thought.

---

[38] A clear effort to supplant Aristotle's *Organon*.

[39] Dampier, W. C. (1929). Op. cit. p. 125.

In their seminal book *Objectivity*, Lorraine Daston and Peter Galison[40] characterize this way of thinking as looking for the "truth in nature"—that is, uncovering inherent, unchanging realities about the world. These cannot be found by observation; their discovery, as with Plato's forms, requires special people with gifted capacities of insight to look beyond the ephemeral as conveyed to us by our (fallible) senses in order to find fundamental and enduring qualities behind appearances; that is the ideal, the "truth" in "truth in nature." And this was the paradigm through which efforts to understand the world were pursued for millennia: gifted observers working assiduously to find the "truth in nature" that is hidden from our perceptions but is, ultimately, what really matters, endures, and is universal.

This worldview was shattered by the emerging technology of the industrial revolution such as the invention of photography, X-rays, and compound microscopes. And almost overnight the neat world of "truth in nature" suddenly became messy. Things that looked identical (like snowflakes) were revealed to differ; effects that seemed symmetrical (like the splashes made when droplets fell into liquids) rarely were. Things that had looked like simple wholes were shown to be composites (e.g., the skin now was understood to consist of cells). John James Audubon's magnificent paintings of dead and artificially posed birds (originally published in 1827),[41] were intended to show the "truth" of their essential qualities; scientifically, however, they could not compete with photographs of living birds taken in natural environments. The methods of "truth in nature" research that produced *ideal-type representations* of what was being investigated were outdone by methods that produced *literal representations*

---

[40] Daston, L. & Galison, P. (2010). *Objectivity*. Zone.

[41] Audubon, J. J. (1840). *Birds of America From Drawings Made in the United States and Their Territories*. J. J. Audubon and B. Chevalier.

of each thing that is examined—a new approach to research that Daston and Galison call *mechanical objectivity*.[42]

Suddenly, scientists of all stripes had to face the disturbing fact that for so long they only had eyes for a perfection that wasn't there. For an illusion. For a manifest fallacy. Recognizing this, they began to look for ways to measure, describe, document, analyze, and understand the world in its full and messy complexity, and to obtain what now was seen as an "objective" view of reality freed from the distorting demands of the search for the perfect, the universal, the ideal type. The key to this new, "mechanical" approach was to *remove as much as possible the presence and distorting subjectivity of the human observer*, the human measurer, the human collector of data, the human interpreter—the program evaluator. The intent was to be as detached as possible in the use of mechanical or, in the case of program evaluations, of highly instrumentalized and proceduralized means (that require minimal judgments by researchers) to collect data—in our case, data consisting of program-based metrics collected in highly manualized and hence replicable ways so that they are both valid and reliable representations of a program and its effects.[43]

But in the end, how useful is limiting our quest for knowledge to the assiduous collection of endless, mechanistically produced data sets? Where does finding infinite variability and nothing more get us? How then can we know what is normal and at what

---

[42] Daston, L. & Galison, P. (2010). Op cit. p. 13.

[43] This reductive version of objectivity sidesteps the problem that any measurement will inherently involve subjective decisions made by the observer, including which among all available data sets should be taken into consideration when evaluating a program. And to put a sharper point on the matter, it obscures the fact that measurement in itself inherently is a subjective undertaking—as many of us experienced during the Covid-19 pandemic when reading the results of our home Covid tests.

point variation tips over from the normal into the abnormal or even pathological? As the 20th century emerged, it became obvious that all these mechanically acquired specimens, these data points collected using highly specified and specific protocols that function in place of human selectivity, ultimately needed to be interpreted. And such interpretation, it was understood, should be assigned to qualified experts—not just to sensitive and intelligent people but to individuals who have gone through the requisite training to be able to draw valid inferences from data.[44]

The age of the experts had arrived and *trained judgment became the accepted means for achieving the best, most objective understanding of the world.* Radiologists, virologists, astronomers, astrophysicists, epidemiologists, neurologists, psychologists, linguists, economists, sociologists, anthropologists, journalists—and program evaluators too—all enjoy our support to the extent that they can give us their best, highly informed interpretations of the world around us. We depend on their judgments, their "objective" understandings to inform our decisions and activities in the muddled world in which we live; and for that matter, we don't much appreciate them when they can't do so crisply and dispositively.[45]

---

[44] This freed us from a dependence on a very few, very intelligent, sensitive individuals like Plato and Aristotle to explain the world to us. It democratized the status of the scientist and the philosopher since potentially, at least, anybody who would apply themselves to the necessary study could become an expert interpreter.

[45] Recall the outcry when the CDC failed to provide crisp, definitive, straightforward, reliable advice on how to contain the spread of the Covid-19 virus. Its experts seem to have focused on providing technically correct information to the point where they lagged behind the public's need for actionable information, and when providing information they seemed not to take into account the societal impact of implementing their suggestions—for example, closing down schools for extended periods without taking into account the damage this might do to children. *This has contributed to a national crisis* as previously respected experts were discredited in a vast swath of the public's mind; and this has fed an already growing distrust of experts and even of science altogether.

Objectivity, then, is a historically contextualized phenomenon that emerged and evolved as part of the tightly interrelated scientific and industrial revolutions in Western Europe, and as a key element of the shift from the paradigms of the Enlightenment into what loosely may be called modernity.[46] As modern researchers, program evaluators are expected to be trained experts who use their knowledge and skills to arrive at valid judgments regarding the nature and effectiveness of the programs they are studying. They are quintessential exemplars of experts using trained judgment, and their methods for collecting and interpreting program data are designed in ways that maximize their plausibility, their claims to objectivity. But can there be, as many people believe, a "gold standard" for doing so?

To answer this question we have to begin by examining *positivism*, the materialist philosophy that provides the foundation for randomized controlled trials (RCTs), which many program evaluators consider the "gold standard" of program impact studies.

The Emergence of Positivism and Its Adoption by the Social Sciences

The term *positivism* was coined by Auguste Comte (1798–1857) who is recognized as one of its founders along with Henri, Compte de Saint-Simon (1760–1825). *Positivism's basic tenet is that only material facts as established through scientific research constitute valid knowledge*—not only for scientists but for philosophers as well. It achieved widespread acceptance in the second half of the nineteenth century and into the century that followed when it

---

[46] It is important to note, however, that as one stage of "objectivity" evolved into the next, older stages did not die out—vestiges remained and can be found even in contemporary thought and research. This will become a critical issue as we delve deeper into impact evaluation as a domain of social epistemology and, more immediately for our concerns, as a way of establishing whether or not a given program achieves what it was intended to accomplish.

actually waned for a while. But in the past few decades, it has been resurrected and scientists in general acknowledge Comte's foundational contributions.[47]

The social sciences arrived on the scene about a century after these so-called "natural sciences" and needed to establish their bona fides for being properly "scientific." Accordingly, it was essential to understand humankind as a part of nature and to look for observable—and measurable—things in terms of which causality in the patterning of social behavior (even deviant behavior), the functioning of social structures, and even the institutionalization of belief systems could be understood.

Emile Durkheim (1858–1917) often is credited with being the "father of sociology." In *The Rules of Sociological Method* published in 1895, he insisted that the cause of any social fact (ranging across the whole spectrum of human behavior from revolutions to the division of labor in society to the application of laws) is to be found by *examining the social facts that precede* it rather than investigating subjective matters such as individual motivations that cannot be observed directly.[48] His study of suicide[49] is among the earliest, and perhaps also the most elegant, use of statistical methods to investigate social phenomena.

It must be said that a major intent behind the adoption of a materialist perspective by early social scientists was, in the spirit of Spinoza, to undercut the theist supernaturalism that had been the West's dominant explanatory paradigm. Instead, they sought

---

[47] Bourdeau, M. (2023). "Auguste Comte." *The Stanford Encyclopedia of Philosophy* (Spring 2023 Edition). Edward N. Zalta & Uri Nodelman (eds.). Accessible at: https://plato.stanford.edu/archives/spr2023/entries/comte/.

[48] Durkheim, E. (1938; orig. pub. 1895). *The Rules of Sociological Method*. The Free Press.

[49] Durkheim, E. (1951; orig. pub. 1897). *Suicide. A Study in Sociology.* The Free Press.

to explain human behavior and to establish a science of society and its constituent parts grounded in observable, aggregated behavioral patterns. In doing so the data of the social sciences would be shifted away from the qualitative findings of ethnographic case studies typical of early anthropology to the "hard" data of a kind whose validity natural scientists would recognize and appreciate. Material social causes would be used to explain social functioning.[50]

Clearly, randomized controlled trials and other evaluation methods that rely on statistical data analysis are the heirs of Durkheim and the epistemic assumptions he made. That this has had significant and not entirely beneficial consequences will become obvious in the discussion of RCTs in Chapter VI and again in Chapter VIII. But first, let's follow the development of positivism and its associated research methods.

Karl Popper—the Formalizer of Modern Science and the Shift from Saint-Simon's Pure Positivism to a Softer Form Called Realism

Karl Popper (1902–1994) is credited by many as the philosopher who formally clarified the fundamental paradigm of modern science. He did so in many books and articles, including *Conjectures and Refutations: The Growth of Scientific Knowledge*[51] and *Objective Knowledge*.[52] As one distinguished scientist put it, "There is no more to science than its method, and there is no more to its method than Popper has said."[53]

---

[50] Harris, M. (1968). *The Rise of Anthropological Theory*. Thomas Y. Crowell.

[51] Popper, K. (1963). Conjectures and Refutations: The Growth of Scientific Knowledge. Routledge and Kegan Paul.

[52] Popper, K. (1972). *Objective Knowledge*. Clarendon Press.

[53] Thornton, S. (2003). "Karl Popper," T*he Stanford Encyclopedia of Philosophy* (Winter Edition), Zalta, N. and Nodelman, U (eds.) Accessible at: https://plato.stanford.edu/archives/win2023/entries/popper/.

If only it were that simple. While Popper quite rightly is thought of as a founder of modern science, as we shall see in Chapter IV the question of what constitutes a scientific research method has, even to this day, not been resolved. In fact, some theorists believe that such a unified view of the scientific method is a goal that can never be achieved.

In any event, Popper took a step back and challenged prevailing scientific practices. Specifically, he contended that it is not enough for a scientific theory to predict events that then are shown to occur. Why? Because many theories are sufficiently vague that any of a wide range of discoveries could serve as representing such predictions, hence could be used to validate them. Indeed, he called theories that don't specify in advance what findings can be used to validate them pseudoscience. This is famously true for psychoanalysis, which he dismissed as a pseudoscience because no matter how a patient's life developed, it could be seen as a validation of psychoanalytic theory—and there was no way to challenge this. But a few years back I found a similar example in my own work when I was asked to consult about a plan to evaluate an after-school program. Its staff claimed that the program (which enrolled middle school students) was "improving the community." Well, any improvement in the neighborhood could be claimed as an instance that validated their program theory—even if the specific improvement they cited (in this case, neighborhood safety) could not be connected to the program's work in any sensible way. My advice to them was: "Don't even bother with an evaluation. Get to work on developing a realistic program logic model, a theory of change."[54]

---

[54] Hunter, D. E. K. (2013). *Working Hard—and Working WELL*. Hunter Consulting, LLC.

Popper dismissed proof by ex post facto validation. Instead, he maintained that instead of relying on after-the-fact validation, a scientific theory must be framed to specify formally *what kinds of findings would disprove or falsify it*[55]. The method is to take the hypothesis that one wants to test and then frame its complete opposite, thereby creating what scientists call the "null" hypothesis. *It is the falsification or disproving of the null hypothesis that proves—for the time being—the validity of the original hypothesis.* Thus, for example, Albert Einstein's general theory of relativity[56] proposing that gravity, far from being an invisible force, is an expression of the curving or warping of space-time by the mass of things occupying it, was very specific about how it could be falsified. By predicting that light passing the sun would be bent toward it, Einstein's theory exemplified what Popper would consider an epitome of good science because it generated a testable null hypothesis—i.e., that in this situation light would not be bent.[57] On the other hand, string theory, or theories about the multiverse (as proposed by some quantum researchers), cannot be falsified and consequently cannot be

---

[55] It is worth noting here that Popper's putting forward of falsification as a research method has become institutionalized among evaluators using randomized control trials through their use of the control group "null hypothesis"—as will be discussed below.

[56] Einstein, A. (1916). "Die Grundlage der allgemeine Relativitätstheorie" [The Basis of the General Theory of Relativity]. *Annalen der Physik*, 49(7): 769–822.

[57] Indeed, Einstein's theory was tested scientifically for the first time three years later in 1919, when the British astronomers Frank Watson Dyson and Arthur Stanley Eddington measured the positions of certain stars in the sky that are closely aligned with the sun and showed, during a complete solar eclipse that made it measurable, how they appeared to be shifting away from the sun as their light was being bent when passing it. Thus they falsified the null hull hypothesis that light would not be bent when passing close by the sun. And although over 100 years have passed since then, Einstein's theory has been validated again and again using similar methods. The fact that replicated studies continued to show the same findings strengthens the theory's truth claims—especially since, as we will see later, replication studies often fail to support original findings (as also noted in the following footnote).

anything more than what Popper would call pseudoscience (at least for the time being) no matter how "scientific" they sound.[58]

Popper went on to caution that the absence of falsifying findings for the null hypothesis does not prove the original hypothesis of a theory is true; rather it allows for the theory to be accepted as true only very provisionally—as a guide to planning new research.[59] This logically leads to the desirability of further testing of the theory and whatever predictive statements this generates.[60] But this can be an infinite series—until pragmatism requires that, in our day-to-day lives and in terms of our conventional thinking, we decide to accept a given theory as "true" and act accordingly. But he insists nevertheless that we should do so only tentatively.[61]

Popper further insisted that scientific research should be objective, by which he meant that research observations and measurements

---

[58] It should be mentioned that there can be an epistemic problem in falsification-based research—namely, lack of agreement on criteria for deciding that a newly discovered fact actually falsifies a theory. This is a major problem in the realm of program evaluations, especially when the intent is to "prove" that a program either "works" or "doesn't work." For example, just because an RCT finds no statistically significant evidence of a program having impact...does that actually mean that that the program's theory of change is wrong, that it "doesn't work"? Not necessarily. It may not "work" in the context in which it was evaluated but in fact be successful in others; it may "work" if and when it is implemented properly; and the research may have been contaminated with aspects that distort its findings—such as observational bias and measurement errors. As a corollary, just because such an evaluation finds statistically significant evidence that a program indeed is having an impact as intended this doesn't mean this will hold for it in other contexts—and, in fact, where such studies are redone they often fail to reproduce the original findings.

[59] Barnes, C. E. (2022). "Prediction versus Accommodation." *The Stanford Encyclopedia of Philosophy. Edward N. Zalta & Uri Nodelman (eds.), Access at:* <https://plato.stanford.edu/archives/win2022/entries/prediction-accommodation/>.

[60] Here is a red flag that we should keep in mind—namely, that very seldom are evaluations of a given program replicated to see if the original finings hold. In fact, I have had evaluators tell me that doing so is a waste of money!

[61] Hacohen, M. H. (2002). *Karl Popper: The Formative Years 1902-1945.* Cambridge University Press.

should be done in studiously neutral ways that come as close as possible to eliminating human judgment as a source of potential bias. In other words, he argued that science should come as close as possible to "mechanical objectivity" that we discussed above. But while it may seem that he fully embraced positivism, this actually was not the case. While he engaged with positivism, he did not embrace it. And he certainly recognized that pure mechanical objectivity is impossible to achieve because all observation takes place within the context of the theory that is being investigated and therefore acts as a filter for what is and isn't observed and measured.[62] In fact, due to the inherently provisional nature of knowledge as he understood it, he considered himself a philosophical *realist*.[63]

Nevertheless, as we shall see in Chapter VI, positivism in its most reductionist form has become deeply established in the use of RCTs to assess the effectiveness of social programs; and their findings often are cited as "proof" that a program does (or doesn't) work. Which, no doubt, has Popper spinning in his grave.

Idealism Reasserts Itself as an Urgent Pushback against Positivism

But the rise of positivism wasn't linear. As the 18th century was left behind European culture morphed into the Romantic Age of the early 19th century. Romanticism, as this movement was known, cut across literature, music, and social thought. With its emphasis on the individual and his or her subjective

---

[62] This subject, often referred to as "confirmation bias," is of importance in program evaluations, and is the core of the difference between positivist RCTs and realist evaluations. Discussions in following chapters illuminate this matter.

[63] Leplin, J. (2011). "Enlisting Popper in the Case for Scientific Realism." *Philosophia Scientiæ* [En ligne], 11. Also seeThornton, S. (2023). Op. cit.

experiences,[64] Romanticism inevitably generated a pushback against positivism—especially in Germany. As one historian of philosophy put it, "It was felt that a critical revision of the foundation of human knowledge was necessary in order to determine the attitude to be adopted towards the new stores accumulated by knowledge."[65]

Perhaps the most influential thinker who drove the movement that bears the name *idealism*[66] was Friedrich Albert Lange (1828–1875). In his widely studied book *The History of Materialism and Critique of Its Contemporary Significance*[67], he argued forcefully that materialism inherently is not up to the task of explaining things, and that what is needed is an epistemic stance that accepts the findings of positivist science but at the same time insists on the need to look beyond them. He contended that all human conceptions of existence must be framed in accordance with the laws of the human mind that are the ultimate basis of all our knowledge.[68] Today Lange is recognized as a leader of the still current "back to Kant" movement.

Is there an epistemic framework that could allow for a bridging of the apparently unbridgeable gulf between positivism and idealism? It seems to me that scientific realism might serve this function.

---

[64] Probably the most famous expression of Romanticism is Goethe's *Die Leiden des Jungen Werther* (*The Sorrows of Young Werther*) which is credited, perhaps metaphorically, with engendering a wave of suicides among lovelorn, bereft young men across Europe.

[65] Höffding, H. (2005). *A History of Modern Philosophy*. Translated from the German by B. E. Meyer. Dover. Vol. 1. p. 541.

[66] A soft idealism, to be sure, in that like Kant he fully accepted the world of substances, of material things.

[67] Lange, A. F. (1866), *Geschichte des Materialismus und Kritik seiner Bedeutung in der Gegenwart*. Iserlohn: J. Baedeker.

[68] Höffding, H. (2005). Op. cit. p. 542.

Scientific Realism—A Bridge
between Idealism and Positivism

What is scientific *realism*? It gained traction by the beginning of the 20th century and can be thought of as resting somewhere between materialistic positivism and idealism. "Scientific realism is a positive epistemic attitude toward the content of our best theories and models, recommending belief in both observable and unobservable aspects of the world described by the sciences."[69]

As we've already discussed, idealism insists that everything we perceive and know about the world has been experienced through our senses and interpreted in—constructed through—our minds. Therefore we can't ever know what exists in the ontological sense of being fully independent of human thought. Realism, in contrast, recognizes a material world that exists independent of human knowledge and experience; and that, over time and through persistent investigation, new aspects of "reality" can in fact be discovered.

Here is a striking example: In 1791 an English parson and philosopher named John Mitchell floated the idea of black holes in our cosmos. This remained conjectural, of course, but also it was taken seriously. Then in his 1915 paper on the General Theory of Relativity[70] Einstein famously predicted that the universe contained many black holes. Still, this was conjectural but again it was taken seriously. Finally, in 1971—a full 200 years after Mitchel had first proposed that black holes exist—evidence of their existence was found by Louise Webster and Paul Murdin

---

[69] Chakravartty, A. (2017). "Scientific Realism." *The Stanford Encyclopedia of Philosophy* (Summer Edition). Zalta, E., N. (ed.). Access at: https://plato.stanford.edu/archives/sum2017/entries/scientific-realism/.

[70] Einstein, A. (1916). "Die Grundlage der allgemeine Relativitätstheorie" [The Basis of the General Theory of Relativity]. Op. cit.

at the Royal Greenwich Observatory and Thomas Bolton at the University of Toronto. Independently of each other, they discovered X-rays radiating from what we now know is a black hole some 5,000 light-years away.

But while supporting the existence of a material world independent of human thought and experience, realism also recognizes how subjective and contextually conditioned such discoveries are.

> Realism holds that there is a real social world but that our knowledge of it is amassed and interpreted (partially and/or imperfectly) via our senses and brain and is filtered through our language, culture and past experience. In other words, realism sees the human agent as suspended in a wider social reality, encountering experiences, opportunities and resources and interpreting and responding to the social world within particular personal, social, historical and cultural frames.[71]

Thus, to restate it, realists accept the materialist view that objects and their characteristics exist independently of whether someone experiences or refers to them. But they reject the ultimate materialist idea that unperceived things cannot be considered meaningfully. All things have inherent properties regardless of what we may think we know about them, the truth of which we may or may not discover.[72] Much of what follows will concern itself with this matter and how it is an important area to explore when considering how to evaluate social programs.

---

[71] Greenhalgh T., Wong G., Jagosh J., Greenhalg, J., Manzano, A., Westhorp G., & Pawson, R. (2015). "Protocol—the RAMESES II study: developing guidance and reporting standards for realist evaluation." *BMJ Open*. 5:e008567.

[72] Moore, G. E. (1963). *Philosophical Papers*. George Allen & Unwin.

In the end, no matter how one thinks about science and its competing epistemic schools of thought, *program evaluation is—and inherently must be—organized around the concept of causality*: predictable consequences flowing from previous events, participant outcomes flowing from their responses to staff activities. Yet causality itself is a problematic idea about which there is a lot of philosophical disagreement.

Chapter III

TIME AND CAUSALITY IN WESTERN EPISTEMOLOGY

Whether one is a positivist or a realist, it is beyond dispute that we need the concept of causality. We are constantly using it without thinking about it. It's essential for living our lives successfully, for planning and making decisions, for everything we do.

Of course, a reliance on causality is fundamental to the design and implementation of social programs. So it is necessary, at this point in our discussion, to interrogate the concept of causality itself, and follow this with a focus on the matter of time—a universal concept that has no universal definition, hence is not at all well understood. Yet, time is an inherent and irreplaceable element of how we understand cause and effect and, much to the point, of any program's logic model or theory of change.

Causality: It's Essential to Evaluating Programs— but Impossible to Know

The challenge of establishing cause-and-effect relationships has been on people's minds at least since Aristotle. In his *Physics* (350 B.C.E.) he maintained that any complete explanation of cause and effect must refer to four factors: (a) *matter*, the substance that changes; (b) *form*, whatever characteristics will emerge from the changes (for programs, their short-term and intermediate outcomes); (c) *an efficient cause*, whatever it is that is inducing the changes (in our case, program activities); and (d) *a final cause*, the long-range benefit of a change. Aristotle's approach is considered teleological—that is, it sees cause and effect as directed in a more or less linear way toward a "final cause" or end, as social programs generally are. For example, a work readiness program will recognize that its participants need to change how they dress when they show up for work (matter); its staff consequently will suggest, and assess, whether indeed their participants are "dressing for success" (form); it will teach the content of a curriculum about appropriate dress in varying contexts (efficient cause); and, (one hopes) it will assess whether participants indeed are succeeding in obtaining and keeping jobs that support the lifestyle they desire (final cause).

Ever since Aristotle, philosophers have debated his "final cause" —which, it is argued by some, is not needed to explain change in the world. Aristotle's counterargument was that while it is not needed to explain change itself it is needed to explain the *regularity* of change, for without a "final cause" there is no source of direction and thus change would be random. *Social programs by their very nature need a posited causal framework that includes specific "final causes" (intended long-term outcomes) to guide their design and implementation to begin with, and then to establish whatever value they add to the lives of their clients over the long haul.* This perspective underlies the well-understood notion that social programs need operational blueprints (theories of change) or logic models to succeed as intended and to be evaluable.[73]

---

[73] Hunter, D. E. K. (2013). Op. cit.

Here it is worth returning to the work of the two 18th century giants of philosophy, the Scottish philosopher David Hume and the German philosopher Immanuel Kant.[74] Hume, the supreme skeptic, argued that it is inherently impossible for us to observe causality at work, that we observe temporal sequences of things and events and impose our mental construct of causality on them—but that causality is a metaphysical concept and consequently at best consists of speculation, and is beyond the realm of what humans can know. This applies even to what many would consider an obvious case of causality: one billiard ball hitting another ball that is at rest, which then begins to move immediately upon impact. Hume claimed that justifying the belief that cause and effect can be observed based on repeated prior experiences (the previous action of the two billiard balls just described) is illogical because attributing causality even in this case requires the assumption that what happens in the future (i.e., in repeated instances) always will be like what happened in the past (not a logically justifiable assumption). Hume's insistence that everything we believe we know about reality—including things causing other things to happen—actually reflects the habits of thinking through which we conceive of the world. As noted earlier, this *idealist position* is very troublesome to most people; and yet it has never been refuted successfully.

Kant, deeply affected by Hume's skeptical argument, nevertheless set out to refute (or at least amend) it. As he put it, "I freely admit that it was the remembrance of David Hume which, many years ago, first interrupted my dogmatic slumber and gave my investigations in the field of speculative philosophy a completely

---

[74] De Pierris, G. and Friedman, M. (2018). "Kant and Hume on Causality," *The tanford Encyclopedia of Philosophy* (Winter Edition). https://plato.stanford.edu/archives/win2018/entries/kant-hume-causality/.

different direction."[75] In his *Prolegomena to Any Future Metaphysics* (1783) Kant agreed that yes, *causality is inherently a mental construct* with its internal logic; but he rescued causality by nudging sideways what Hume had said. Causality, he argued, while an a priori mental category, is not something we impose de novo on each experience. Rather, we use the concept of causality to structure our experiences in the first place. We simply can't see a billiard ball hitting a stationary one that starts to move immediately upon the collision without regarding it as an instance of causality. In this way, our understanding of causality grows out of our experiences. It is tied to them, not imposed on them.

But that's not enough. Kant insisted additionally that a true statement of cause and effect must be broader. It must include the condition that each such observed occasion must be a particular instance of a general, universal, and unchanging "law of nature." Thus the case of the billiard balls is a specific instance manifesting Isaac Newton's first law of motion (that an object will not change its motion or lack of it unless an external force is applied to it)—which is a generally accepted universal "law of nature." But while for Kant our use of cause and effect ultimately has a material basis such as Newton's first law, our *experience* of any worldly instance of causality (as we have when watching a game of billiards) is entirely a mental phenomenon.

In the case of program evaluations, this means that claiming a program is causing impacts requires not just Aristotle's four factors (matter, form, efficient cause, and final cause). One also must include reference to whatever research has established as universally effective ways for human beings to influence each other, and specify which of these the program is using to promote desired

---

[75] Ibid.

changes in its participants—for example, using an incentive system that rewards the adoption of desired behaviors in a partial hospital program for individuals with psychiatric disorders. As we will see in Chapter IX, this means looking beyond program components or elements into the mechanisms that stimulate changes in program participants—that is, produce outcomes. (We will be considering the concept of mechanisms at some depth in Chapter X.)

Kant's modified idealist perspective on causality continues to be influential. After all, we live in a world that we define by place and time, by sequences of actions enacted in particular contexts at particular moments. Programs work in specific venues with en-rolled participants, and participants achieve outcomes (we hope). Cause and effect, before and after, in temporal sequences. Which means that time, as we experience it, is an essential factor when we think about causality.

Time and Causality

Already in the 6th century B.C.E. the issue of time and causal-ity was a bone of contention among Greek philosophers. At stake was what about our lived experiences is real; specifically, whether the way we experience the world consists of illusory convictions about cause and effect that we use continuously to navigate life.[76]

Plato elaborated on these considerations when he suggested that the true essences of things, their forms, are timeless—but that the world of human experience is changeable and as a consequence is inherently defined at least in part by time. For Aristotle as well, time was more or less identical with motion (change). And so things stood, in various iterations, until the late 17th century

---

[76] Benjamin, C. (1966). "Ideas of Time in the History of Philosophy." In Fraser, J. T. (Ed.) (1966) *The Voices of Time*. George Braziller. pp. 3-30. p. 9.

when Isaac Newton (1642–1727) identified two versions of time: (1) what we might call the "objective" version of time that is true and absolute, omnipresent and all-pervasive, and proceeds along without relationship to anything else[77]; and (2) our "subjective" time, or *duration*, which is always relative to the succession of our perceptions—hence motion—and gives us such things as minutes, hours, days, years, and so on.[78] Kant, acknowledging that time is a very confusing matter, agreed with Newton that objective time exists independent of any content, but rejected the idea that it can exist independently outside the human mind.[79]

Speaking practically, it is fair to say that in general humans perceive time in terms of four aspects: (1) we identify and live inescapably in—are eternally trapped in—what we call the "present moment"[80]; (2) we remember things from the past, i.e., before the present; (3) we anticipate what will happen in the future, i.e., whatever will follow the present moment; and (4) whatever time is, *it doesn't seem to us to stand still*—it is dynamic, ever in flux, and unidirectional (time cannot be reversed).[81]

---

[77] This conception of time as absolute and ubiquitous ultimately was refuted in 1905 by Einstein in his Special Theory of Relativity. Time "dilates"—it actually speeds up or slows down for a given entity in relationship to its speed of travel as measured from a separate platform, through what now is called space-time. See: Einstein, A. (1905). "Über einen die Erzeugung und Verwandlung des Lichtes betreffenden heuristischen Gesichtspunkt" [On a Heuristic Viewpoint Concerning the Production and Transformation of Light]. *Annalen der Physik*. Vierte Folge (in German). Johann Ambrosius Barth.

[78] Benjamin, C. (1966) Op.cit.

[79] Ibid. pp. 17-23.

[80] Although it must be emphasized that we have no way to capture the length of time that a present moment occupies.

[81] Except in the domain of quantum mechanics where time actually is reversible. See, e.g., Emery, N., Markosian, N., & Sullivan, N. (2020). "Time." *The Stanford Encyclopedia of Philosophy* (Winter Edition). Edward N. Zalta (ed.), URL = <https://plato.stanford.edu/archives/win2020/entries/time/>.

Ultimately, time—in both its "objective" and "subjective" aspects—is a mental construct. It is a very short and seamless story we tell ourselves constantly over and over again, unthinkingly, and in an utterly compelling manner as we relate to the world.[82] It defies any widely accepted definition, and yet it is a fundamental element of what we call causality. This is the basis for holding that causality is beyond what humans can prove and therefore is a metaphysical concept.

How, then, can we deal with cause and effect in program evaluations? The only way is to substitute the operational (numerically based) laws of probability for the commonly invoked metaphysical[83] laws of causality.

Why is this important? Because it means that t*he causal assumptions underlying program evaluations cannot be "proven" in any absolute or universal sense—and more importantly, neither can their findings.* So of necessity we operate within the framework of probabilities as best we can. We go about observing and measuring what we construe to be the essential aspects of programs and their elements and then infer whether and to what degree a given program is likely to produce results or impacts as intended. This pragmatic approach is fine as far as it goes. But it becomes highly problematic when, as discussed above, RCTs, or evaluations of any kind, are seen as dispositive regarding "what works."

Accordingly, although we might wish otherwise, there can't be a universally right method for evaluating program effects. The methods that are selected must depend greatly on the nature of the question(s) to be answered and consequently, what is to be examined.

---

[82] Hossenfelder, S. (2022). Op. cit.

[83] Again, causality is a metaphysical concept because it cannot be measured and hence is outside the realm of science. Hossenfelder (see previous footnote) considers such concepts "ascientific."

"When dealing with different accounts of causation, it is important to understand that different accounts explain the nature, essence, or ontology of causality in different ways. On this fundamental level, they define causality differently and offer different explanations of what causality is."[84]

Put another way, program evaluations investigate contextualized and emergent phenomena; their findings inherently will be incomplete and provisional.[85] It may be hard to accept this thought, but in the end, we must acknowledge that program evaluations are not exercises in discovering the "truth" about how well a program is performing. Rather, at best, they tell us what is plausibly true to us regarding the effects of a program—true in terms of our beliefs and expectations about the world—that is, in terms of our (rarely examined) epistemic worldview. Evaluations, while wrapped in the mantle of scientific objectivity, in no way are capable of discovering inherent (ontological) truth. This is why Bruno de Finetti, a leading theoretician about the nature of probability, argued that it does not exist in the world external to the person who makes calculations about it. Such calculations, he insisted, are subjective quantifications about the degree of uncertainty that the individual feels about a given eventuality. They are, therefore, no more real than cosmic ether, unicorns, or witches.[86]

To summarize so far: Statements about the causation of program outcomes and impacts are not statements that in an ultimate

---

[84] Palenberg, M. A. (2023). "Causal Claims in Contribution Analysis." *Canadian Journal of Program Evaluation*. Vol. 37.3 (special issue):389-402. p. 392.

[85] As Popper argued, this is true for all areas of human inquiry. Consider, for example how data from the James Webb Space Telescope at this very moment (January 2024) are blowing up the "Big Bang" theory about the origin of our universe and along with it some of our basic understandings of cosmological physics.

[86] De Filetti, B. (1977). *Theory of Probability Vols. I and 2*. Wiley.

sense can be "proven," nor can they be "true"—rather, they are statements that have been developed and presented in ways that make them plausible to us, statements we are persuaded are right, statements that we decide to trust, that we can believe are true. They are rhetorical statements—not statements of ultimate truth or ontological fact. And so, rhetoric itself is the topic of the next chapter.

Chapter IV

EVALUATION METHODS AS RHETORIC

In his *Rhetoric*,[87] Aristotle developed his ideas on how to make effective speeches. However, he was less interested in analyzing specific methods than in arguing that an effective speaker should be able to assess his or her audience and understand what kinds of arguments will be persuasive to its members, and to frame the contents of an intended speech accordingly. Not that skilled rhetoric will be able to persuade all people all the time. But mastery of rhetoric will persuade one's audience (or at least a good portion of one's audience) of the plausibility—including the value—of whatever is being presented or discussed. So Aristotle does not see good rhetoric as a way of developing new knowledge through dialogue (which was Plato's approach). To Aristotle, it is a way of persuading people to adopt the speaker's views.

Which is exactly what program evaluators must be able to do—why would anybody pay for an evaluation whose findings, good or bad, will not be accepted as plausible? And toward this end, the evaluation profession has adopted professional standards of practice. These standards are intended to increase the likelihood

---

[87] This was written in at least two periods, though the dates remain uncertain. The first period was while he was associated with Plato's academy 367–347 B.C.E., and the second 335–322 B.C.E. when he had his own school, the Lyceum.

that their findings will be accepted as "objectively true" representations of a program and its results. Said differently, they are devices for allaying reservations about evaluative findings that inevitably are the product of a series of what, as we have seen above, in part are ascientific, metaphysical assumptions and subjective interpretations.

So, it seems to me fair and reasonable to view evaluations as devices of rhetoric: They are designed to produce plausible findings but are repurposed in many instances as claims of causal truth.

Putting it this way may seem pretty cynical or even radical and, in all likelihood, many people—including many evaluators—will experience this statement as such. But in fact, this view aligns fully with the contemporary paradigm for "objectivity" (discussed in Chapter II)—namely, that *objectivity in modern usage refers to judgments made by trained experts.*

"Does the program work?" often is the bottom-line question that evaluators are asked to answer. It is a question that has two elements: causation and probability. And since, as discussed in Chapter III, *causation is a metaphysical concept that inherently can't be proven*, the issue will always boil down to the second element—probability. As it was put in a paper by respected evaluators, this "creates the paradox that commissioners of impact evaluations pose legitimate but unanswerable questions, and impact evaluations need a way to reconcile the impossible with the possible."[88]

But before delving deeper into evaluation methods with their inherent strengths and weaknesses, it seems reasonable to consider the more basic matter of science, and specifically the question of

---

[88] Ton, G., Mayne, J., Delahais, T., Morell, J., Befani, B., Apgar, M. & O'Flynn, P. (2019). "Contribution analysis and estimating the size of effects: Can we reconcile the possible with the impossible?" *CDI Practice Paper 20*. Centre for Development Impact.

whether in fact there is something that could be called the scientific method. Why? Because the widely held notions regarding what science is and what it can achieve strongly influence how we respond to efforts such as program evaluations that are dressed in what we might call "scientific garb."

Chapter V

LOOKING FOR A SCIENTIFIC METHOD: INSTRUMENTALISM VERSUS ESSENTIALISM

Generally speaking, it is widely accepted that there is a fundamental and universally applied *scientific method*—a way of looking at and developing knowledge about the world. Although people may use different terms to describe it, they more or less agree that the scientific method consists of some version of the following: (a) observing the world, (b) selecting aspects of it on which to focus, (c) developing theories about its nature in these specific domains, (d) producing hypotheses to test these theories, (e) doing research that either supports or disproves the validity of each hypothesis, (f) revising theories as indicated by what research has discovered…and (g) then restarting the cycle. Science in this description is grounded in what can be observed, is iterative, and produces inherently provisional knowledge.

The only problem with this view is that it's wrong!

There is, in fact, no agreement among scientific thinkers about what a universal scientific method is,[89] *nor even what sets science apart, definitively, from pseudo-science and other ways of developing*

---

[89] Hepburn, B. & Andersen, H. (2021). "Scientific Method." *The Stanford Encyclopedia of Philosophy.* (Summer edition) Edward N. Zalta (ed.), URL = <https://plato.stanford.edu/archives/sum2021/entries/scientific-method/>.

knowledge.[90] Space prohibits delving into the enormous literature on research methods, so I will confine myself to considering two of the more prominent views of science that currently hold sway: instrumentalism and essentialism.

Both instrumentalism and essentialism have their roots in a fight among philosophers in Germany during the late 19th century. This fight was started by Johann Gustav Droysen[91] and extended a bit later by Wilhelm Dilthey.[92] They both were intent on legitimating the study of the humanities against the claims of the natural sciences, which had become the prevailing approach to discovering "truth" and explaining it. Droysen and Dilthey called the aim of natural science *erklären* (which translates into English as "to explain"). Against *erklären* they put forward the concept of *verstehen* ("to understand"), which requires a deeper look at things and the meanings human beings place on them.[93] In this dichotomy, which subsequently was brought into the social sciences by Max Weber,[94] those people interested in "erklären" work within an instrumentalist framework, those interested in "verstehen" within an essentialist one.

Instrumentalism

The instrumentalist perspective sees science, its theories, and its calculations as a toolbox for making predictions about events that

---

[90] Hansson, S. O. (2021). "Science and Pseudo-Science." *The Stanford Encyclopedia of Philosophy*. (Fall Edition), Edward N. Zalta (ed.), URL = <https://plato.stanford.edu/archives/fall2021/entries/pseudo-science/>.

[91] Droysen, J. G. (1867). *Grundriss der Historik*. Veit.

[92] Dilthey, G. (1883). *Einleitung in die Geisteswissenschaften*. Dunker & Humblot.

[93] Apel, K-O. The Erklären-Verstehen controversy in the philosophy of the natural and human sciences. In: Fløistad G. (Ed.). *La Philosophie Contemporaine/Contemporary philosophy. International Institute of Philosophy* / Institut International de Philosophie, vol 2. Springer. pp. 19-49.

[94] Weber, M. (1958/1905). Op.cit.

subsequently will emerge. Science seen in this way is instrumental in that it has no other purpose than making such predictions and testing whether they are accurate. This may seem straightforward, but actually has far-reaching implications. For example, in discussing instrumentalism Popper[95] uses the case of Galileo Galilei (1564–1642), who famously invented the telescope and, among other things, explained that what appears to us as the sun's daily travel around the earth is, in reality, due to the earth's rotation on its axis as it travels around the sun. After some debate, the Church was willing to concede that Galileo's explanation made calculations of the movement of heavenly bodies simpler and more reliable, and therefore accepted his framework for making such calculations by choosing to understand it instrumentally (to use our terminology). But Galileo did not stop there. He took the next step and insisted that what he was proposing was not merely a refined tool for making measurements and calculations but rather that it constituted a new description of what is true about the nature of things. For this essentialist heresy, the Church tried and under threat of torture forced Galileo to recant his claim that he had achieved a new and improved understanding of reality, and to announce publicly his adoption of the Church's instrumentalist stance that allowed the universe to continue peacefully along rotating around the earth. (But he did so, it is said, muttering unhappy soto voce demurrals all the way.)

A more contemporary and famous example of how pure instrumentalism can dominate scientific thought is the exchange between Albert Einstein and the Danish physicist Niels Bohr at the 1927 Solvay Conference about quantum mechanics.[96] To Einstein's

---

[95] Popper, K. (1963). Op. cit. pp. 130-133.

[96] Caroll, S. (2019). *Something Deeply Hidden: Quantum Worlds and the Emergence of Spacetime*. Dutton.

dismay, Bohr and his German colleagues Werner Heisenberg and Wolfgang Pauli insisted that the only legitimate facts of science are those that can be observed or measured, and that there is nothing of interest to be said beyond them. The object of science, in their view (often referred to as the Copenhagen School of Thought), is not to understand what the world is, nor to have theories about what exists, but is only to calculate and make predictions about what new observations and measurements will find given a set of initial conditions. Einstein was appalled and took the opposite (essentialist) position, namely that science should always strive to understand the world and how it works. He argued for Kant's position that it is our theories about what exists that organize and direct what we decide to measure, and these theories can take into account what might be true even though nothing so far has been observed or measured to substantiate them. Generally speaking, the scientific establishment decided that Einstein had lost this argument and quantum research adopted the instrumentalist perspective—enjoining researchers to quit trying to understand things and to "Shut up and calculate!"[97] Only recently has this view been challenged. Once again serious scientists are arguing that science should indeed seek to explain what the world is and how it works, not merely make predictions about what new observations will reveal under given conditions.[98]

This debate, although it may appear to be remote, has direct implications for program evaluations. Instrumental evaluations such as RCTs test whether a program is producing measured results as intended (a matter discussed in some detail in Chapter VI).

[97] N. David Merman apparently is the author of this phrase characterizing the Copenhagen School of thought, although often it is attributed to Richard Feynman.

[98] Becker, A. (2018). *What is Real?* John Murray.

They make use of research protocols using metrics that standardize the collection of data and reduce as much as possible human judgment in finding results. In other words, their approach to objectivity is mechanical, consciously designed to minimize as much as possible human subjectivity (see Chapter II). They identify initial or so-called baseline conditions for program enrollees, then make predictions about how they are likely to look in terms of measurements to be taken after they have completed the program (if a set of protocols is adhered to with fidelity). They embody the "Shut up and calculate!" perspective. They don't, however, illuminate *why* a program works (or doesn't), *how* a program works (or doesn't), *where* it works (or doesn't), and *for whom* it works (or doesn't). To answer those kinds of questions—in other words, to *understand* a program—we need something else entirely: namely, essentialist evaluations.

Essentialism

All things that human beings recognize—things they think about, value, and use—they organize by classifying them into categories (e.g., as mountains, rivers, program participants, program activities). All categories rely on one or more characteristics through which members of a given category are grouped together and understood to be distinct from all other things. Our culture, and more specifically the language we speak, generates and depends on such groupings. These groupings, and the symbols that represent them, organize our experience of the world and without them, we would be stuck—unable to think, to act, to know what to do or how to do it. Indeed, as a species, we wouldn't even be human.[99]

---

[99] Geertz, C. (1973). *The Interpretation of Cultures*. Basic Books.

All culturally meaningful categories have two kinds of characteristics: (1) essential features their members must have to be included, and (2) accidental features that they may or may not exhibit while belonging to that category. Essentialist thinking requires that researchers look behind easily observable phenomena to the "reality," the essences, the essential features that lie behind them.[100] For program evaluators intent on understanding a program beyond documenting its activities and results, this means looking beyond them and asking generative questions such as "Through what mechanisms does the program actually work?" or "How do the characteristics of the organization that is providing the program influence program effectiveness?" and so on.

Unlike the easily observed and quantifiable program elements described in instrumentalist program evaluations such as RCTs, what essentialist program evaluators search for often is more or less invisible and rather hard to identify let alone quantify. Yet (as will be discussed in Chapter IX) this is exactly what so-called "realist" program evaluators actually attempt to do. For such studies, objectivity depends not on mechanical standardization and quantification of procedures but rather on the interpretive abilities of trained evaluators to make sense of hard-to-find and hard-to-measure program essences. Indeed, some theoreticians would argue that it is the essences of a program that constitute what the program really is.[101]

---

[100] Becker, A. (2018). Op. cit. pp. 139-144.

[101] Fine, K. (1994). "Essence and Modality: The Second Philosophical Perspectives Lecture", *Philosophical Perspectives*, 8:1–16.

Chapter VI

INSTRUMENTALISM MADE OPERATIONAL: POSITIVISM AND RANDOMIZED CONTROLLED TRIALS

While there are many options for evaluating programs and their impacts, each with its pros and cons, in this chapter I will look at *positivism and the use of randomized control trials* (RTCs) because this is the dominant approach for program impact studies in the U.S. Many other kinds of program evaluations such as benchmarking studies, quasi-experimental studies, and rapid cycle studies are not discussed here because they all tend to work within a positivist philosophy along with RCTs, and so considering them would not help clarify the epistemic issues that are the main concern of this book. For similar reasons, consideration of so-called "mixed methods" that involve both quantitative and qualitative approaches is deferred to Chapter XIII.

How RCTs Evaluate Programs

Michael Scriven,[102] a hugely influential mathematician, philosopher, and evaluator is widely credited with bringing RCTs

---

[102] Scriven, M. (1982). *Logic of Evaluation*. EdgePress; and Scriven, M (1987). *Theory and Practice of Evaluation*. EdgePress.

to American program evaluation during the late 1950s and early '60s. He did so with a focus on the areas of health services and education. Generally speaking, Scriven limited his evaluations to looking at the characteristics of participants entering what came to be called the program's "black box," and then at the outcomes that could be measured for participants who finished their program (who left the "black box")—*but without ever looking inside the box itself.* So Scriven's approach to RCTs could only claim to identify impacts—but not explain how or why they were caused.[103] These beginnings have shaped the design of RCTs to this day.

Fundamentally, RCTs rely on two means to understand what programs are accomplishing: (a) a *successionist perspective*, in which whatever causes something must precede its effects: first there is a program, then there are its outcomes; and (b) a *counterfactual method* that relies on the comparison of program participants' outcomes with those of a control group composed of people who are as closely as possible identical to the program participants in terms of demographic and risk indicators. Let's look at these approaches a bit more deeply.

RCT Methods of Analysis

As many readers will know, RCTs rely on the *experimental method*. They evaluate program impacts in the following way: A large pool of individuals who meet the eligibility requirements of a given program are divided into two groups on a random basis so that their relevant profile characteristics such as age, gender, ethnicity, and risk factors are evenly distributed across both groups. One group is then enrolled in the program and is the so-called

---

[103] Scriven, M. (1987). Ibid.

test or *proband group*; the other group (the so-called *control group*) becomes the basis for assessing the null hypothesis[104] or, to use the lingo of evaluation, it becomes the counterfactual for the test group. After some time, both groups are assessed for the presence of those participant changes the program is intended to produce—i.e., the program's outcomes. The difference between these groups in the prevalence and/or size of such changes is the basis for deciding how effective a program is—that is, whether it is producing impacts at a statistically significant level.

The statistical assumptions and methods used will be discussed in the following chapter. Here it is worth emphasizing that RCT research methods are very well developed and are governed by *institutionalized, explicit quality standards regarding operational matters* such as randomization, sampling, using validated measurement tools, and the ways in which analyses should be conducted. Therefore, it is possible to assess a given study against these operational norms and form an opinion of its quality and the meaning of its findings. Using these well-understood standards, RCT evaluators rely principally on *deduction* to look at the categories of data they have assembled and then draw conclusions about the causal relationships between them (e.g., the relationship between program activities on the one hand, and participant outcomes on the other).

---

[104] Following Popper (see Chapter II) scientists are in agreement that it is useless to try to prove, and impossible to disprove or falsify, the hypothesis one wants to test—which in our case would be that the program in question is producing outcomes effectively. So for such research one creates a so-called null hypothesis—that is, a statement contrary to the original hypothesis that a given program is effective; it posits that there is no statistically significant difference between outcomes for the test group and those for the control group. If a statistically significant difference between these groups' outcomes is found to exist, this would falsify or "disprove" the null hypothesis—which then is taken as "proving" (or at least validating) the original hypothesis, namely that the program is producing outcomes as intended.

By virtue of the use of RCT methods to establish their impacts, programs with statistically significant results are widely heralded for their effectiveness. But why? The answer is that program evaluation was inspired and informed by—indeed emerged from—the methods of the natural sciences, which value "quantitative measures, experimental design, and statistical analysis as the epitome of 'good' science."[105] Undoubtedly, this is a very powerful reason why program evaluators and the practitioners, funders, policymakers, and pundits who use and advocate for RCTs have adopted this methodology as the "gold standard" for impact evaluations. "Good" science is just so damned believable!

However, a big caveat is in order. Rarely mentioned is the fact that in *transporting RCTs from the natural sciences to the evaluation of social programs the use of the double-blind method—one of the essential elements of scientific RCTs—was left behind*. What are double-blind methods? Let's use the medical testing of newly developed drugs as an example. In a double-blind RCT to evaluate the effectiveness and risk factors of medicines, neither the patients who are given the medication nor those who are given a placebo (which is designed to have no medical consequences), know whether they are in the test group that is getting the medicine or in the control group that is not. Furthermore, and this is key, *the researchers don't know either*. Thus double-blinding eliminates a dangerous kind of bias from evaluations—namely, that those who perform them can, perhaps without conscious intent, distort their findings in the direction of confirming that the medicine is both safe and effective.[106]

---

[105] Patton, M. Q . (2008). Op. cit. p. 423.

[106] Sadly, as will be discussed more fully below, a fair number of medical RCTs involve the intentional manipulating of data to favor a given medication; it would be pollyannaish to think such manipulations don't ever occur in our domain. See Ioannidis, J. P. A. (2005). "Why Most Published Research Findings are False." *PloS Medicine*. 2(8)e124. pp. 0696-0701.

Naturally, it is inherently impossible for the evaluations of social programs to be double-blinded: the program participants know full well that they are in the program, the members of the control group know full well that they have been excluded from the program, and the researchers who study both groups know full well which is which. *So the rigor of RCT studies in the natural sciences inevitably is watered down when RCT methods are imported to evaluate social programs.* But this has not prevented consumers of what must be considered the fundamentally enfeebled RCT evaluations of social programs from wrapping them in the cloak of scientific credibility. And because few stakeholders seem to be aware of this watering down of RCTs when they are used to evaluate social programs, this evaluation method enjoys widespread acceptance as the "gold standard" for studying program impacts.

However, even leaving aside the lack of double-blinding, other factors can raise questions about an RCT evaluation's findings.

> Unlike many biomedical experiments, in which everyone in the experimental group actually receives the pill or the vaccine, in a social experiment, everyone is offered the program but not everyone will actually participate. Some people in the experimental group will come by for the first session and drop out; others will come occasionally; and others will come regularly. This is part of the treatment. Some people in the control group will find a different program. If they are not chosen for the treatment program, some will go elsewhere and join a different activity.... Since it is often the case that some members of the control group receive some kind of somewhat similar service, findings of program impact are weaker than they would be if the control group did not receive any services.[107]

---

[107] Moore, K. A. & Metz, A. (2008). "Random Assignment Evaluation Studies: A Guide for Out-of-School Time Program practitioners." *Research-to-Results. Part 5 in a Series on Practical Evaluation Methods*. p. 4.

So the fact is that life is messy and its vagaries can insinuate themselves into program evaluations. In some instances, the findings will appear stronger than they may be; in some cases, weaker. This problem manifests itself in diverse ways even though RCTs do, in fact, eliminate some major kinds of research bias that are known to occur in social program evaluations.

RCTs Control for Major Biases in Program Evaluations

There are three kinds of bias that RCTs generally can eliminate: selection bias, maturational bias, and historical bias.[108]

Selection bias

This bias comes about when the enrollment process (wittingly or unwittingly) recruits many participants who already have achieved the intended program benefits before they were enrolled—or who have a better-than-average likelihood of achieving them. A case in point: I was asked to review a program in the U.K. intended to improve high school graduation rates for children who showed key risk factors for dropping out of school prematurely. But when I looked closely at the program, it turned out that program staff in the schools were deliberately recruiting students who were highly likely to graduate. They did so because they knew the program as designed couldn't possibly work for marginal students who were at risk of dropping out. Why? Because staff members each carried a caseload of about 100 students and, at the same time, were expected to meet management's demand for an 80 percent high school graduation rate. This, the staff knew, was impossible to achieve

---

[108] Gordon Berlin, one of America's leading evaluation methodologists, helpfully suggested that I focus on these sources of bias during conversations regarding RCTs (2023).

with a caseload that large. Simply put, here we had a supercharged example of what often is called "skimming" or "creaming"—selection bias on steroids. *Selection bias is exactly what the randomized selection process built into all RCTs is designed to neutralize—and does very well.*

Maturational bias

This bias is seen when outcomes that are attributed to a program really would have come about even without it, simply as a fact of human development. So for example, young people in a youth development program lasting several years often will become more thoughtful over that time period because that's what happens normally with adolescents. If the program selects improved thoughtfulness for its outcome, it is biasing its so-called results massively toward success—and undercutting its claims of program effectiveness. Unless, of course, members of the counterfactual group inexplicably do not become more thoughtful. *The use of a counterfactual by RCTs provides an effective means to neutralize maturational bias.*

Historical bias

This bias exists when contextual factors change significantly during the time that a program is being evaluated, and these changes significantly improve or diminish participants' likelihood of achieving intended outcomes. For example, a prison release (reentry) program that shows declining rates for reincarceration among its graduates could simply be benefiting from the well-documented drop in national crime rates over the past thirty years. Or consider the fact that while crime rates did start to fall in the 1990s after the Clinton administration funded an increase in police officers nationwide, they continued to fall even when the number of police officers started dropping again. So while advocates of "law and order" policies such as increasing police may point to falling crime rates as an outcome of this policy, serious evaluators and policy analysts have refuted their assertions and shown that the drop in crime rates was caused by the confluence of multiple historical variables—and that no single policy or approach or program drove it. *Here too, the use of a counterfactual is designed to neutralize this form of bias.*

Clearly, when done well randomization and the use of a counterfactual largely remove major kinds of research bias. But not all. They can't mitigate the effects of other forms of bias such as *confirmation bias*, one of the most important sources of bias when researchers know which group is the program group and which is the control group and, as mentioned above, in the course of making their outcome measurements, may tend to rate members of the test group more favorably. Confirmation bias is especially a risk where the evaluator already believes in the program's effectiveness (for example, when the evaluator also was the program's original designer). The problem persists in program RCTs because they inherently cannot be double-blinded, which is the most reliable way to manage confirmation bias.

Nor does randomization itself eliminate another source of bias that emerges when, as can happen, there are differential attrition rates in the test and control groups. This can lead to a skewing of the demographic and risk profiles of these groups, and consequently of the outcomes being examined. Furthermore, members of the two groups may interact and one group may influence members of the other group in ways the evaluators might not capture—which can lead to changes in the test group mistakenly being attributed to the effects of the program.[109]

Finally, although it isn't exactly a form of bias, there is the problem *that observation and measurement in themselves can distort research significantly.* While this is not often discussed outside the realm of quantum mechanics, this problem also manifests itself in program evaluations: regardless of specific evaluation methods used by the evaluator, the very act of observing can change what is being observed.[110] This phenomenon was first discovered by researchers who were studying worker productivity at the Western Electric telephone manufacturing factory in Hawthorne, Illinois between 1924 and 1933. What happened is that simply placing observers in selected work areas resulted in increased productivity—which subsequently has come to be known as the "Hawthorne Effect." While this was a very disquieting discovery and has been controversial ever since, a review of nineteen research projects studying behavioral changes by participants in response to being studied[111] concluded that consequences "of research participation for behaviors being investigated do exist, although little can be securely known about the conditions under which they operate, their mechanisms of effects, or their magnitudes."[112]

Worth noting here is the fact that what could be called "observation-introduced bias," and especially confirmation bias, were

---

[109] Befani, B. (2012). "Models of Causality and Causal Inference." A working paper that contributed to Stern, E., Stame, M., Mayne, J., Forss, K., Davides, R. & Befani, B. (2012) *Broadening the Range of Designs and Methods for Impact Evaluations.* Working aper 38. Department for International Development. P. 17.

[110] Befani, B. (2012). Ibid.

[111] McCambridge, J., Witton, J. & Elbourne, D. (2014). "Systematic review of the Hawthorne effect: New Concepts are needed to study research participation effects. *Journal of Clinical Epidemiology.* Vol. 67(3):267-277.

[112] Ibid. p. 267.

of sufficiently great concern to Michael Scriven that he proposed a rather controversial way to limit them—namely to undertake "goals-free" evaluations that look at program participants' needs and measure everything that could conceivably represent a positive change.[113] Such a scattershot approach, he argued, also would promote the discovery of unanticipated effects and thereby broaden what can be learned from an evaluation. Of course, the more outcomes that are measured, the greater the possibility that the evaluator will hit on one that is a "false positive" and never know it yet claim it as evidence of the program's success (as is discussed in the following chapter). Alternatively, such a "discovered" outcome, even if not a "false" positive, may be used to claim a program's "success" even though this outcome never was what the program was intended to produce. In fact, changing the evaluation of what is to be considered a program outcome mid-stream in an evaluation is not all that unusual, and generally happens when the evaluator, often under pressure from program leaders or funders, is effectively looking for any way possible to validate the program in cases when the expected pattern of outcomes is failing to emerge in the course of the evaluation—a kind of confirmation bias that is hard to discover since the failure to find outcomes as originally intended often is not mentioned in the final, somewhat deceptively positive report.[114]

How RCTs Deal with Causality

RCTs are understood to be most useful in situations where the program being evaluated is relatively straightforward, with simple

---

[113] Scriven, M. (1972). "Pros and Cons about Goal-Free Evaluation." *Evaluation Comment: The Journal of Educational Evaluation.* 3(4):1-7.

[114] Ritchie, S. (2020). *Science Fictions: How FRAUD, BIAS, NEGLIGENCE and HYPE Undermine the Search for Truth.* Metropolitan Books.

(and few) cause-and-effect assumptions underlying the program design.[115] A corollary of this, as the medical research methodologist John Ioannidis points out, is that *the greater the number of program elements, and the lesser the number of previously validated elements used to design a program—the less likely the evaluation findings are to be a good reflection of "reality."*[116] With this caveat, let's look at how RCTs deal with causality.

A very useful article[117] on causation lists four major approaches to causation, of which RCT methods rely on two: a counterfactual approach and a successionist approach.

The Counterfactual Approach to Causation

As has been shown, RCTs are inherently concerned with those changes that appear among program participants versus what happens with members of the counterfactual group; and this method is, as discussed above, a powerful tool for eliminating or at least managing down important sources of bias. However, RCTs do not focus on which components of a program are inherently necessary or sufficient to produce outcomes—or to use the categories discussed above, which are essential and which are accidental.[118] Nor do they explore *how* and *why* the program may have contributed to the outcomes. So it is important to understand that RCTs, like

---

[115] Perrin, B., Speer, S., Saunders, M., Stame, N., Stern, E. & Ofrir, Z. (2007). *EES Statement: The importance of a methodologically diverse approach to impact evaluation—specifically with respect to development aid and development interventions.* European Evaluation Society.

[116] Ioannidis, J. P. A. (2005). "Why Most Published Research Findings are False." *PloS Medicine.* 2(8)e124. pp. 0696-0701.

[117] Palenberg, M. A. (2023). Op cit.

[118] In fairness it must be recognized that some RCT evaluations do attempt to discover which program elements are most strongly driving outcomes; they do so by relying on statistical means—e.g., ex post facto regression analyses.

any evaluative approach, make compromises about what they will and won't examine, the questions they will and won't answer. They are positivist in that they focus only on what can be observed and measured about program participants, the program components that are provided to them, and the outcomes that these participants achieve. They are not designed to explore intangibles or to improve our *understanding* of programs. This point will become clearer when we discuss the mechanisms through which programs change participants—a central interest of "realist" evaluations (see Chapter IX).

The Successionist Approach to Causation

RCTs take a strictly linear approach to causation.[119] They rely on observing two consistently manifested, co-appearing things where "entity C" (cause) always precedes "entity E" (effects)—and the corollary that every time one observes an "entity E" that one will have observed an "entity C" that preceded it. Here C consists of a program and its elements, as delivered via program activities to program participants. E stands for the changes manifested by the program participants. If C always precedes E, then the successionist assumption is that the program caused the observed changes in the participants, thus giving these changes the status of program outcomes. While this is how we generally think in our daily lives, nevertheless this logic has its limitations. It ignores contextual influences and indeed encourages the belief that programs with "proven" outcomes can easily be transported from one context

---

[119] Befani, B. (2012). "Models of Causality and Causal Inference." A working paper that contributed to Stern, E., Stame, M., Mayne, J., Forss, K., Davides, R. & Befani, B. (2012). *Broadening the Range of Designs and Methods for Impact Evaluations*. Working Paper 38. Department for International Development.

to another—that is, that their findings are generalizable. Which is simply not true (see Chapter VIII).

Inevitably, all approaches to evaluating the results of a given program will have to make assumptions about, and find some way of analyzing, the likelihood that their findings are something more than an artifact of chance—that is, that they are very probable and thus a useful way of representing reality as we can know it. RCTs, embedded as they are in a positivist view of the world, rely perhaps more than other evaluation methods on the determination of the level of statistical probability that characterizes their findings; that is, on statistical significance.

But what makes for statistical significance? We will consider that next.

Chapter VII

THE SIGNIFICANCE
OF STATISTICAL SIGNIFICANCE

Pierre Simon, Marquis de Laplace (1749–1827) was the most prominent of the 18th-century thinkers who were developing and formalizing theories of probability. Not only did he publish important academic essays on probability, he also sought to educate the public about this concept. It was toward this end that he published his *Essai philosophique sur les probobilités*[120] in 1796. And he had a compelling reason for doing so. As he put it, "Strictly speaking it may…be said that nearly all our knowledge is problematical[121]; and in the small number of things which we are able to know with certainty, even in the mathematical sciences themselves, the principal means for ascertaining truth—induction and analogy—are based on probabilities; that the entire system of human knowledge is connected with the theory set forth in this essay."[122]

This statement contains two beliefs that still characterize probability theory. The first is that it provides us with the means "for ascertaining truth"; the second is that virtually all knowledge is

---

[120] Simon, P. (1951 [1796]). *A Philosophical Essay on Probabilities*. Dover Publications.

[121] It is possible that what he meant here is "probabilistic."

[122] Ibid. pp. 1-2.

a matter of probability. Since in general usage the word "truth" denotes a sense of certainty about what is known, simultaneously claiming that virtually all knowledge is a matter of probability introduces what in epistemic terms certainly is a profound muddle; and this accounts, I believe, for the fuzzy use of language and associated disarrayed thought when RCT findings are presented as "the truth" about program impacts (as discussed in earlier chapters). To understand why this is so, it is worthwhile to explore the notion of statistical significance, that aspect of the theory of probability that is most relevant for program evaluations.

RCTs and the Concept of Statistical Significance

Perhaps the most widely made assumption in RCTs is that for an evaluation finding to be valid the statistical probability of its being "true" must be 95 percent or better. This standard was adopted and popularized by the British geneticist and mathematician Ronald A. Fischer (1890—1962), whom many consider to be the father of modern statistics and whose 1925 seminal book *Statistical Methods for Research Workers*[123] has set the standard for evaluators.

Operationally, this is an application of Popper's insistence that rather than looking to confirm a hypothesis, science can only work by falsifying the logical negative of the original hypothesis, that is, the *null hypothesis*. How can the null hypothesis be falsified? By arriving at findings that could not exist if it were true. In program evaluations, this standard requires evaluators to articulate a clear

---

[123] Currently available in a compilation of three of his books: Fischer, R. A. (1990). *Statistical Methods, Experimental Design, and Scientific Inference*. A Re-issue of *Statistical Methods for Research Workers, The Design of Experiments*, and *Statistical Methods and Scientific Inference*. 1st Edition edited by J. H. Bennet. Oxford University Press.

hypothesis about the program's ability to produce effects as desired, then develop a null hypothesis positing the opposite—i.e., that the program can't produce its intended outcomes. So, when the evaluation indeed identifies and measures program outcomes as originally posited, this falsifies the null hypothesis. The falsification of the null hypothesis is how the original hypothesis—that the program can and does produce outcomes as intended—can be accepted as scientifically valid.

More specifically, to "prove" a program's impact, the RCT data should show that it is the program that makes the difference—that there is a five percent chance or less that desired outcomes would occur naturally for program participants, even without the program, seen in the light of what happens to members of the control group. Evaluators call this calculation of probability the *p-value* (short for probability value), and a p-value of less than or equal to 0.05 is the generally recognized standard (originally proposed by Fischer) for accepting that the program has produced the measured outcomes (which consequently are called impacts). In this way, the effectiveness of the program is held to have been "proven"[124]—or at least established beyond a reasonable doubt.[125]

So, let's review the history of this standard. Fischer built on the previous work of Jerzy Neyman and Egon Pearson in their article "On the Problem of the Most Efficient Tests of Statistical

---

[124] Readers may want to see this at play on the website of the What Works Clearing House operated by the U.S. Department of Education's Institute of Education Sciences. https://ies.ed.gov/ncee/wwc/whoweare. Here "what works" is defined as having statistically significant RCT evaluation results—that is, a p-value equal to or smaller than 0.05.

[125] And it certainly is worth noting that adoption and (rigid) adherence to the p-value standard inevitably will lead to ignoring other information, at least some of which will likely be important. See the section on "toxic positivism" which follows shortly.

Hypotheses" published in 1933.[126] They reasoned that while one never could be sure whether the results of an experiment (or, the matter that concerns us, a program evaluation) proved anything, one nevertheless could limit the chance of mistakenly concluding that an experiment or a program had produced positive results when subsequently results from replicated studies could show that actually there were none (called a "false positive" Type I error). Or, on the other hand, mistakenly concluding that there were no positive results when indeed it turns out that there were (a "false negative" or a Type II error). Their approach proposed an analytical standard that promised researchers that their conclusions would more often be correct than wrong. *Notice: there's no promise made that in any given case the findings would either be true or not, wrong or not.* And yet, public policy-makers, private funders, program operators, performance management consultants, and even evaluators "hype" programs when they claim that they have been "proven" to work because their RCT findings are statistically significant if their p-value is less than or equal to 0.05.

It bears restating: Use of a p-value is never a way to prove truth; it is a defense against an excess of false positives due to random outcomes that might otherwise be regarded as "true." The use of a p-value of 0.05 or less to claim that research results are "statistically significant" is a matter of convention. There are, however, researchers who are very concerned about the pervasive use of the p-value of 0.05 as the "make or break" standard for claiming statistical significance.[127] In fact, "scientists and statisticians have

---

[126] Neyman J. and Pearson, E. S. (1933). "On the Problem of the Most Efficient Tests of Statistical Hypotheses." *Transactions of the Royal Society of London. Series A, Containing Papers of a Mathematical or Physical Character* 231 IX. pp. 289–337.

[127] Dushoff, J., Kain, M. P. & Bolker, B. M. (2019). "I Can See Clearly Now: Reinterpreting Statistical Significance." *Methods in Ecology and Evolution*. Vol. 10. January. pp. 756-759.

bemoaned the shortcomings of null hypothesis significance test-ing for nearly a century"[128] and there are calls for diminishing the reliance upon, or even abandoning, the use of the p-value. Instead, they call for concentrating on the *size of effects* (rather than their level of statistical significance) and on *confidence intervals* (that is, the range within which findings will be deemed important). They also note a foundational problem with the use of the p-value in the social arena where it is almost impossible for the null effects that are posited in a null hypothesis to have a value of zero, which is the necessary underlying assumption of significance testing based on the p-value.[129]

It is these considerations that have driven the proposal to cease using the term statistical "significance" at all. Instead, the authors argue, researchers should describe the results of their null hypothesis tests in terms of their statistical "clarity."[130] Why? Be-cause this language reminds us that the data of a statistical anal-ysis are merely that: data. By saying the data provide clarity, it is almost impossible to ignore the follow-up question: "Clarity about what?" And then we are talking about what scientists call the "system" but for our purposes would be the program itself. Thus it is very relevant that, as we know well, the vast majori-ty of social programs produce effects of modest social value at best. Indeed, surprisingly few social programs, when rigorously evaluated, are found to produce the hoped-for improvements in participants' lives.[131] And this sad fact, rather than the data them-selves, should be our main concern if the evaluation of social

---

[128] Ibid. p. 756.

[129] Ibid.

[130] Ibid.

[131] See: "Evidence Based Programs—Social Programs That Work.".Accessible at: https//www.evidencebasedprograms.org./.

programs is to contribute to the enhancement of our society by helping to strengthen the programs meant to improve the lives and prospects of their intended beneficiaries.[132]

But What is Probability?

Generally speaking, when we talk about probability we are dealing with uncertainty; we are interested in the likelihood of some event transpiring—say that individuals participating in a program will achieve specific outcomes. It turns out, however, that there are two fundamentally different ways of interpreting uncertainty, of considering probability: *frequentist* and *Bayesian*. Let's look at them in turn.

Frequentist Probability

The usual way of conceiving frequentist probability is the familiar coin flip. The idea being that an evenly balanced coin with heads on one side and tails on the other has, with any fair flip, a 50 percent probability of landing on heads and a 50 percent probability of landing on tails. But we all know that if we flip a coin just a few times, we might get a disproportionate number of

---

[132] However, some notable exceptions test the rule as in the case of the Nurse-Family Partnership (NFP). This program provides home visitation services by specially trained APRNs for low income, first time mothers. And repeatedly across all sites with different contexts as well as differing ethnic groups, RCTs have documented that NFP in fact does produce life-changing results both for the mother and for her child: for the mother, better pregnancy outcomes, reduced abuse of her child, deferred second pregnancy, less time spent on government assistance, reduction in arrests, and increase in months employed; for the father, greater presence and involvement in parenting; and for the child, reduction in delayed language development, better school readiness, better school performance, at age fifteen better school attendance, and reduced involvement in criminal behavior. See e.g.: Olds D. L. & Kitzman H. (1993) "Review of research on home visiting for pregnant women and parents of young children." *The Future of Children*. Vol. 3. pp. 53–92; Olds D. L., Henderson C. R. Jr & Kitzman H. (1994). "Does prenatal and infancy nurse home visitation have enduring effects on qualities of parental caregiving and child health at 25 to 50 months of life?" *Pediatrics*. Vol. 93. pp. 89–98.

heads (or tails). *So what we are really talking about here is long-term frequency*—as when, for example, the coin is flipped 1,000 times. The expected result would be that a showing for both heads and tails would cluster very close to 50 percent—so-called *regression to the mean*. The basic assumption is that each flip of the coin will have identical variables such as the force of the flip, the height of the flip, the number of rotations of the flip, etc. This is fine, perhaps, when talking about coin flipping. But how does this apply to program evaluations?

In program evaluations, the issue is not so much how many times one measures a phenomenon as in flips of a coin. Rather, the issue is the number of participants. The more participants, and hence the higher the statistical power of the evaluation, the more confidence we have that results are not false negatives and the more stock we can put in a study's findings. But, since most social programs are relatively small and the fact that one needs hundreds of participants for an adequate power value, many evaluations will lack a sufficiently high statistical power to give us much confidence in their findings even when these are "statistically significant" at a p-value of 0.05 or less.

The frequentist approach is entirely concerned with data, is deductive, and is predictive regarding them: it assigns probability to new data that will be forthcoming. It is wholly positivist in its approach, leaving little room for subjectivity. The analytical methods used by frequentist evaluators are *independent of prior knowledge about the kind of program being evaluated*, highly formalized and, if they meet professional standards, leave very little to interpretation. Thus they are understood to be as close as possible to the kind of "mechanical objectivity" that was discussed in Chapter II.

Also, the frequentist approach is based on the assumption of perfect replicability. But is this way of looking at things really sensible when talking about social programs? As one author puts it, "[o]ur conclusions regarding null and alternative hypotheses presuppose the idea that we could conduct the same study an infinite number of times under perfectly reproducible conditions."[133] But nothing about human beings and their institutions ever is static, unchanging, or perfectly reproducible. So in the case of RCT evaluations, although we would like to think that the calculated p-value is a powerful standard for assessing the likelihood that data about future outcomes will be achieved as intended, this is a hard belief to defend when we move from the realm of the theoretical to the untidy realities of the quotidian. And it should not surprise us, therefore, that when RCTs are replicated for a given program they are more than likely not to show the same results.[134]

Bayesian Probability

Named after the English statistician, philosopher, and minister Thomas Bayes (1702-1761), Bayes' theorem argues for a method to update looking at probabilities that is based on currently available data and past knowledge. *In contrast to the frequentist approach where future data are a variable whose probable distribution is to be predicted, in Bayesian analyses parameters and hypotheses themselves are seen as probability distributions and the data as fixed.*[135] Thus,

---

[133] Kaplan, D. (2024). *Bayesian Statistics for the Social Sciences.* 2nd edition. Guilford Press. p. 6.

[134] Lehrer, J. (2010). "The Truth Wears Off." *The New Yorker*, December 13. pp. 52-57.

[135] Fornacon-Wood, I., Hitesh, M., Johnson-Hart, C., Faivre-Finn, C., O'Connor, J. P. B. & Price, G. J. (2022) . "Understanding the Differences Between Bayesian and Frequentist Statistics." *International Journal of Radiation Oncology. Biology. Physics.* Vol. 112, No. 5, pp. 1076–1082. Published by Elsevier Inc. All rights reserved. https://doi.org/10.1016/j.ijrobp.2021.12.011. p. 1076.

unlike frequentist thinking where probabilities are assigned to forthcoming data, Bayesian thinking assigns probabilities to how validly hypotheses reflect present reality, how well they describe what currently is happening in a program, and therefore how well they are likely to predict what will happen (e.g., that a program's participants will achieve targeted outcomes as intended). Said differently, "Bayesian models incorporate prior knowledge into the analysis, updating the probable accuracy of hypotheses as more data become available."[136]

What would a Bayesian analysis of a social program look like? Among other things, the prior knowledge it would examine could consist of known research on pertinent topics, relevant available program evaluation reports, the opinions of highly regarded experts in applicable fields, and the experiences of people from backgrounds similar to those of program participants. *Bayesian evaluators work inductively (generalizing from prior knowledge) to produce hypotheses and models for understanding programs and then use them to predict actual outcomes however they can be discovered— not predefined data sets about them.*

To be clear: Bayesian research is inherently an iterative process, where initial hypotheses based on prior knowledge are tested against available and accruing evidence, then reformulated as indicated, then tested again for as long as seems wise. Thus, *unlike with frequentist evaluations such as RCTs, not only is interpretation and hence subjectivity built in, it is fundamental to the approach.* Consequently, this kind of probability is variously referred to as "subjective probability" and "epistemic probability." Indeed, in his foundational work *Theory of*

---

[136] Fornacon-Wood, I., Hitesh, M., Johnson-Hart, C., Faivre-Finn, C., O'Connor, J. P. B. & Price, G. J. (2022). Ibid.

probability Vols. I and 2,[137] Bruno de Filetti argued that "only subjective probabilities exist—i.e. the degree of belief in the occurrence of an event attributed by a given person at a given instant with a given set of information."[138] Thus according to de Filetti, *probability calculations say nothing about the world as it is, but rather reflect the degree of our uncertainties and beliefs about the world around us.*

Bayesian objectivity is a product of disciplined and informed interpretation, the most recent approach to objectivity as discussed earlier in Chapter II. As will be shown in Chapter IX, this line of reasoning underlies so-called "realist" evaluations, the major alternative to RCTs discussed in this book.

Should We Trust the Findings of a Single RCT with Statistically Significant Results?

Well…no! At least not uncritically.

Let's look at it this way. If you have 100 programs that have been evaluated for their impacts using RCTs and all have a p-value equal to or less than 0.05, then it is very likely that five out of these hundred programs will not be producing impacts as claimed. Which translates into one out of every twenty. They will represent "false positives"—so-called Type I errors. Of course, it is impossible to know which ones represent Type I errors, yet stakeholders in each program will claim their program has been proven effective, proven to work. *This is why research methodologists understand that one RCT alone is not very meaningful and that we should only begin to trust their findings when the evaluation has been duplicated under the same conditions, with the same profile of*

---

[137] De Filetti, B. (1977). *Theory of Probability Vols. I and 2*. Wiley.

[138] Cited in Kaplan, D. (2024). Op. cit. p. 6.

participants, and with the same interventions[139]—something which is not very realistic and rarely happens.[140]

As was mentioned above, when efforts are made to reproduce the findings of an RCT, it is extremely unusual for them to succeed in reproducing the findings of the original evaluation. As one article puts it, "The truth wears off."[141] Or as the medical researcher and research theoretician John P. Ioannidis puts it so pithily and succinctly: "Most Published Research Findings are False."[142]

Ioannidis lists six things that can affect the probability that a research finding is "true"—true, that is when truth is defined in terms of the statistical significance of research findings.[143] I quote them here as he lists them and add comments after each:

1. *The smaller the studies conducted in a scientific field, the less likely the research findings are to be true.* [Comment: Where in a given field studies tend to be small and thus less powerful, the prevailing knowledge base will reflect this and be relatively weak—which in general is true of programs in the social sector.]

2. *The smaller the effect sizes in a scientific field, the less likely the research findings are to be true.* [Comment: This is highly pertinent in the domain of social programs which, as was discussed above, typically produce relatively small effect sizes.]

---

[139] Public Library of Science. (2007). "Is Most Published Research Really False?." ScienceDaily. 27 February. Access at: www.sciencedaily.com/releases/2007/02/070227105745.htm.

[140] One approach to dealing with this problem is to conduct meta-analyses of multiple RCT studies. This is discussed in Chapter X.

[141] Lehrer, J. (2010). Op. cit.

[142] Ioannidis, J. P. (2005). Op. cit.

[143] Ibid. pp. 0697-0699.

3. *The greater the number and the lesser the selection of tested relationships in a scientific field, the less likely the research findings are to be true.* [Comment: Again, highly relevant to the evaluation of social programs since there are so many different kinds of programs and so many different groups of intended beneficiaries—while at the same time, relatively speaking, such a very small number of programs have been evaluated.]

4. *The greater the flexibility in designs, definitions, outcomes, and analytical modes in a scientific field, the less likely the research findings are to be true.* [Comment: This describes very well the state of evaluations in the social domain.]

5. *The greater the financial and other interests and prejudices in a scientific field, the less likely the research findings are to be true.* [Comment: In my view, the field of social programs is rife with vested financial interests as well as doggedly held and insisted upon beliefs about "what works" that amount to prejudices. Why? Social programs rarely earn enough to support their work and therefore rely on support from private funders (who typically have strongly held and frequently sentimentally grounded beliefs), foundations (which often are doing research to find validation for their programs and initiatives rather than with a stance of genuine curiosity), and government (which has a stake in proving the value of its efforts to the voting public).]

6. *The "hotter" a scientific field (with more scientific teams involved), the less likely that the research findings will be true.* [Comment: This may seem paradoxical, but Ioannidis explains it this way: The more evaluations that are being produced at the same time in a given domain, the higher the priority becomes for stakeholders

to disseminate their most impressive "positive" results. Here we see the poisonous effects of publication bias, which will be discussed shortly.]

Ioannidis discusses three things that are needed to produce evidence that indeed it is highly probable that a program is producing effects as intended: (1) the prior probability of its being true (as determined before doing the study—e.g., doing a Bayesian analysis); (2) a low level of its p-value (less than 0.05); and (3) the statistical power of the study. These points have already been discussed. But with regard to the first it is worth stating explicitly: what this means is that *programs are more likely to be "proven" effective if it is highly probable that they are effective.* So here we are talking about two probabilities and using one probability (the likelihood that the program *will* produce impacts) to predict another (the likelihood that the program indeed is producing them). But if the first probability makes the second probability likely, it is at least worth asking ourselves whether the cost in time, money, and effort to get to the second probability really is worthwhile. And the circular reasoning is hard to overlook: That a finding is more likely to be true if evidence predicts that it is likely to be true.

Arguing, as he did two decades ago, that there is enormous pressure on researchers to achieve p-values at or below 0.05 to get their studies published in reputable journals and that much of what does get published is false,[144] Ioannidis was a prophet. But he was by no means a false prophet. Indeed, what Ioannidis was anticipating is what I consider the birth of a cult—the cult of the p-value.

---

[144] Ioannidis, J. P. (2005). Op. cit.

Toxic Positivism: The Cult of the P-Value

To state the obvious: The basic fact of life for researchers, including program evaluators, is that unless they can get their work published they will be relegated to the margins of their profession—not only in terms of their status but also in terms of their access to major funding sources. *And p-value is the foremost screen through which scientific papers must pass to get published.*

Again, let's turn to Ioannidis who states flatly:

Several methodologists have pointed out that the high rate of nonreplication (lack of confirmation) of research discoveries is a consequence of the convenient, yet ill-founded strategy of claiming conclusive research findings solely on the basis of a single study assessed by formal statistical significance, typically for a p-value of less than 0.05. *Research is not most appropriately represented and summarized by p-values, but, unfortunately, there is a widespread notion that…research articles should be interpreted based only on p-values*[145] (emphasis added).

In a world as it should be, all research reports that reflect high professional standards would get published. This would make it possible for us to build our knowledge based on what we learn regardless of whether the findings in a given case are positive or negative. Screening for publication would consist of benchmarking all studies in terms of how well they conform to practice standards and decidedly not screening them based on their conclusions. In this world, one would expect the corpus of all published studies to include a large number of reports where results did not meet the stakeholders' original hopes and expectations, but that contribute meaningfully to our knowledge base.

---

[145] Ibid. pp. 0697-0699.

Sadly, that's not the reality of the world in which we live. In fact, studies of published research show, against all odds, an extraordinary preponderance of reports that tell only of positive findings.[146]

> Understandably, editors and referees are biased against papers that report negative results; they greatly prefer positive, statistically significant results. Researchers know this and often do not even submit negative studies—the so-called 'file drawer effect.' Once enough nominally positive confirmatory papers appear the claim becomes canonized, making it even more difficult to publish an article that reports a contrary result. This distressing tendency happens in the media as well, which amplifies the misinformation.[147]

This situation is called *publication bias*. Journal editors and reviewers are likely to publish papers that are interesting and preferably groundbreaking. So they are looking at the results a paper reports and rarely at the methods by which they were achieved. But what they do look at, indeed often to the exclusion of other selection criteria, is the p-value of the reported results. Researchers know this of course, and stack the deck so their papers are more likely to be published. They do so in various ways, some of which include outright fraud where data are literally manufactured out of thin air or are knowingly "corrected."[148] One method, as suggested

---

[146] Fanelli, D. (2011). "Negative Results are Disappearing from Most Disciplines and Countries." Sociometrics. Vol. 90(2). March. pp. 891-904.

[147] Miller, H. I. & Young, S. S. (2024). "The Validity of Much Published Scientific Research is Questionable (Part 1)." American Council on Science and Health (acsh.org) https://www.acsh.org/news/2024/02/20/validity-much-published-scientific-research-questionable-part-1-17449.

[148] Ritchie, S. (2020). Op. cit. Suart Ritchie is a Scottish research psychologist who, since 2018, has been on the faculty of the Institute of Psychiatry, Psychology, and Neuroscience at Kings College in London. In 2021 his book *Science Fictions: How FRAUD, BIAS, NEGLIGENCE and HYPE Undermine the Search for Truth* was nominated for the Royal Society Prize for Science Books.

in the previous quote, is simply to avoid doing replication studies of previous RCTs because journals tend not to publish them, preferring to present "new" research(which, really, is a form of self-censorship). There is also an insidious form of self-censorship where researchers (and we have no reason to doubt that this will include some program evaluators) actually avoid taking on projects where the likelihood of attaining positive results with adequate p-values seems minimal; rather, to please journal editors they look for likely "winners" on which to build their careers.

As we know, Ronald Fischer promulgated the now universally accepted standard that evaluations should achieve a p-value of 0.05 or less if their findings are to be sufficiently credible. He did so intending to eliminate or at least reduce subjective distortions in research findings. The theory was reasonable—but as the saying goes, "There's many a slip 'twixt the cup and the lip!" *And the biggest "slip" is this: Achieving a p-value of 0.05 has become the most important goal for many researchers—at times even more important than whether the findings are true.*

This fact has generated a new kind of pathological behavior called p-hacking—that is, contriving to get one's study to a p-value of 0.05 or less by virtually any means possible. It is only inevitable that if one tries in enough ways to achieve a desired statistical result this will indeed emerge simply as a statistical artifact—and will generally be a Type I error.[149] Or consider the practice of looking for extra data if one's findings have a p-value above 0.05. As soon as the new data are found that get the value to 0.05 or lower, data gathering is stopped—ignoring the possibility that further

---

[149] This is because the finding is a statistical artifact alone, not a result of credible data being analyzed in good faith. Hence, it is more than likely that such an exercise will yield a "false positive."

data gathering could once again yield a higher, less significant p-value; there's just no way of knowing. That this matter amounts to a massive crisis for science across the board is well documented, as in the recent book by Stuart Ritchie, mentioned above. He reports that over the last couple of decades *tens of thousands of published reports of RCT-based studies have been retracted in the natural and social sciences because, in retrospect, their findings have proven to be deceptive*: due (a) to outright fraud; (b) confirmation bias; (c) sloppy or neglectful research methods; or (d) unjustified post-publication hype.

A case in point: A recent research integrity study in Holland[150] found that over 50 percent of Dutch scientists "regularly engage in questionable research practices, such as hiding flaws in their research design or selectively citing literature...[and] one in 12 admitted to committing a more serious form of research misconduct within the past three years: the fabrication or falsification of research results." Not surprisingly, it found that pressure to publish was "most strongly correlated with questionable research behavior."

And so here we have the "cult of the p-value" that has arisen due to the interplay between the frantic pursuit of the low p-value in research findings on the one hand, and the iron fist of publication bias that insists on a 0.05 p-value or lower on the other.

Researchers are only too aware of these issues and many responsible evaluators caution repeatedly against accepting any given RCT as "proof" that a program or intervention "works" even when the probability that it is producing effects as intended has a p-value of

---

[150] De Vrieze, J. (2021) "Landmark Research Integrity Survey Finds Questionable Practices Are Surprisingly Common." *Scienceinsider. Science*. July. Access at: https://www.science.org/content/article/landmark-research-integrity-survey-finds-questionable-practices-are-surprisingly-common.

0.05 or less.[151] The most obvious solution, of course, would be to replicate impact evaluations of a given social program at least once if not several times as is the standard practice for medical research—a standard, Ioannidis suggests, that even in that domain often is not met. For social programs, it bears repeating: such replicated evaluations are few and far between.

The Ghost of Laplace Still Haunts Us

RCT findings often are treated as dispositively true—as the ultimate basis for making decisions about the worthiness of programs: Are they worth funding or continuing to support? Should they be scaled up or replicated? Should they be closed down? Are they doing much good, or enough good to justify their cost? Or are they actually doing harm, affecting participants' lives negatively? We need to answer such questions as best we can. To do so it is essential to choose a frame of reference and way of thinking—an epistemology —and an associated evaluation methodology. And as just stated, at least in the U.S., the overwhelming tendency is to rely on the epistemic school of positivism and the associated evaluation methods of RCTs.

Indeed, the U.S. Department of Education's Institute of Education Sciences (I.E.S.) has explicitly adopted RCTs as the accepted means for producing what it considers to be the highest level of evidence for the effectiveness of education programs. It ranks evaluation efforts accordingly in its What Works Clearinghouse,[152] where the highest credibility is given to RCTs—especially when

---

[151] I am especially indebted to Gordon Berlin, research professor at Georgetown University and former president of MDRC, for making this point very strenuously in a personal communication to me when commenting on an earlier draft of this manuscript (April 2023).

[152] What Works Clearinghouse. Access at: https://ies.ed.gov/ncee/wwc/.

there are multiple evaluations of a given kind of program that can be studied using statistical meta-analyses (see Chapter XI). In fact, the I.E.S. not only wants to see statistically significant evidence of effectiveness as measured by quantified impacts, it also prefers to see statistically significant findings for program impacts from prior efficacy[153] research on the program. As the I.E.S. puts it:

> Effectiveness Research should be justified by strong empirical evidence of the efficacy of the intervention, as demonstrated by *statistically significant and substantively important estimates* of impact, from one study that includes multiple sites or settings, or two studies that each include one site or setting, all of which meet the guidelines for evidence to be produced by Impact Research…or evidence that the intervention is widely used even though it has not been adequately evaluated for efficacy.[154] [155]

The Campbell Collaborative,[156] an international body of health and social service researchers, also has adopted RCTs as the best credible source of information on program effectiveness. So too, the

---

[153] In the I.E.S.'s terms, program *efficacy* is established through RCT studies under "ideal conditions" where, among other things, program developers provide significantly more than normal ongoing support to program implementers in order to ensure that the program is delivered with high fidelity to the original design. Program *effectiveness* is established through RCTs where the program is implemented with minimal support from the developers and consequently the level of fidelity to the original program design is likely to be more flexible—which is to say, the way the program actually is delivered "on the ground."

[154] Institution of Education Sciences. (2013). *Common Guidelines for Education Rsearch and Development*. U.S. Department of Education and the National Science Foundation.

[155] In the normal course of things, very few programs meet this standard. Rarely is a social program's efficacy studied before its effectiveness is researched, and rarely is a given program evaluated more than once.

[156] https://www.campbellcollaboration.org/ Named after Donald T. Campbell (1916-1996), a member of the American National Academy of Sciences who believed that scientific research should be utilized to assess the effectiveness of government programs and reforms.

Coalition for Evidence-Based Policy[157], which explicitly considers RCTs the only valid impact evaluation method. And the Cochran Library,[158] which collects and reviews "high quality, independent evidence to inform healthcare decision-making"[159] clearly favors research using RCT methods. All, however, also emphasize the importance of synthetic meta-analyses that look across families of similar programs to identify more reliably "what works." This topic is explored rather fully in Chapter XI.

Well, the ghost of Laplace encourages us to believe that RCTs with statistically significant findings are discovering "the truth." And generally speaking, at least in the social sector, advocates, pundits, funders, and practitioners tend to believe this and assert that this is so. Furthermore, in my experience, so too do many evaluators—at least in public where they have stakeholders to satisfy.

Given the importance and high credibility our society attaches to RCT findings, we must understand some noteworthy issues about their beliefs and assumptions, as well as the methods that are rooted in them—to which we turn next.

---

[157] One of the Coalition's key concepts is that "Programs meeting the highest standards for proven effectiveness should receive top priority for funding." (emphasis added) Accessible at: https://www.evidencebasedpolicy.org/.

[158] Cochrane Library. Access at: https://www.cochranelibrary.com/.

[159] See: https://www.cochranelibrary.com/about/about-cochrane-library.

Chapter VIII

SOME NOTEWORTHY ISSUES REGARDING RCTs

As with any evaluation method, RCTs have their own set of epistemic issues. In their case, it seems to me that some of the problematic assumptions and methods discussed in this chapter can be traced back around 2,700 years to the static epistemology of Parmenides, whom we met in Chapter I.

RCTs Have a Limited "Cause and Effect" Methodology

We can begin with a general matter: the linear "cause and effect" methodology of RCTs makes them suitable only for evaluating relatively simple interventions in relatively simple situations where the context can be expected to play a minimal role in the program's effectiveness. This refers to situations, where absent effective intervention, both the program and the counterfactual group can reasonably be expected to change little throughout the evaluation.[160] One might well wonder how often such circumstances present themselves.

Conceiving of Programs as Bounded Entities Constructed Out of Discrete Parts

More concretely, there is the matter of how programs are conceived of as objects to be evaluated. In the case of RCTs, programs

---

[160] Perrin, B., Speer, S., Saunders, M., Stame, N., Stern, E. & Ofrir, Z. (2007). Op.cit.

are conceived of categorically—that is, as constructed out of relatively unchanging constituent parts or elements, which together belong to a clearly bounded social entity: the program has an identifiable location in space and time and it is clear what constitutes the program and what lies outside it.[161]

Let's look at how this plays out on the ground. **Turn90,**[162] a program in South Carolina that helps people transitioning out of incarceration to reintegrate into their communities, consists of four elements: (1) classes in cognitive behavioral therapy; (2) transitional work; (3) supportive case management services; and (4) job placement upon completion of the program.[163] In an RCT evaluation, these four program components would be described in terms of the activities they entail and who provides them, and treated like beads on a string that make up a necklace—the **Turn90** program. The program, seen as a bounded entity that is to be described in terms of its static elements, would then be discovered to be effective—or not.[164]

But as practitioners know full well, programs bring into themselves many external (contextual) variables beyond those accounted for with "treatment as usual" assumptions (discussed below). These include such things as the lived experiences of staff; preconceptions or biases held by employees about program participants (which can lead them to be either overly optimistic or overly pessimistic about being able to help them achieve intended outcomes); to what degree

---

[161] In this regard it is worth mentioning that putting things into categories means deciding what criteria will be used to do so and, consequently, not paying attention to other matters. Or, as has been known at least since Aristotle, categorization requires simplification.

[162] I worked with **Turn90** on their original theory of change.

[163] See: https://turnninety.com/our-approach/.

[164] As of this date **Turn90** has not yet undertaken an impact evaluation that meets RCT standards. However, it is assiduously tracking outcomes for program graduates that suggest the program is producing good results.

staff do or don't "look like" program participants; organizational stresses or even organizational dysfunctions that influence program delivery (not unusual, for instance, when new administrative or executive staff are hired or when funding is cut); and on and on. So then, how bounded are programs really? In point of fact, as any social scientist understands, *there is no such thing as a closed human system; all human systems—including social service programs—have permeable boundaries.*

Where do we draw a program's boundaries, where do we build a wall and say we will only consider what's inside it, what's contained, what's (relatively) easy to observe, describe, measure, and interpret? Program operators, their funders, their staff, and even their program participants come to tacit agreements about these matters and, often without much thought, accept these agreements as "real" descriptions about the way things are, what the program "is." Then, those who evaluate program impacts help to reify these unexamined agreements—which by their nature are reductive and as such are simplifications that structure what is evaluated. While it can be argued that all scientific inquiry necessitates simplifications of some sort, it seems to me that it is the task of evaluators to spell out the "what and why" of the simplification built into their evaluation plan and the consequent limitations of what can be learned. And this I have rarely seen done.

To summarize, RCTs tend to look at programs as bounded entities that can be evaluated in a more or less static and decontextualized way. While this allows for a kind of easy-to-manage neatness and supports relatively simple data collection and analysis, it is also quite disconnected from the way we understand the world in which we live, and to which we adapt as best we can. As I see it, RCTs often present findings that are precise—but spuriously so.

Forced Dichotomization of Results
that Really Are On a Continuum

For decades, evaluators have recognized that how RCTs analyze outcomes is deficient in a number of ways: "These deficiencies include the dichotomization of results that are on a continuum; inaccurate interpretation of results that are not statistically significant as supporting the null hypothesis; incentive to alter the analysis to attain statistical significance; and loss of important details about the magnitude, pattern, and precision of observed associations."[165] In other words, as was discussed in the previous chapter, reliance on the p-value forces an "all or nothing" perspective: if the p-value is greater than 0.05, a program's effectiveness will likely be questioned.

But the world is far more complex than this picture. We should keep in mind that p-values are averages and don't tell us about variations within a group; what programs can and do accomplish will vary among participants, just the way school students will vary among each other in how well and how much they learn. This point often is missed entirely when stakeholders discuss whether a program "works." As discussed in Chapter VII, this would be less likely to happen if we were to discuss program effects in terms of statistical clarity rather than statistical significance.

The realities of programs, as for much of life, are much more nuanced and diverse, and ignoring findings with high p-values deprives us of the opportunity to learn a great deal about program design, participant selection and enrollment, program delivery, how

---

[165] Savitz, D. A., Wise, L. A., Bond, J. C., Hatch, E. E., Ncube, C. N., Wesselink, A. K., Willis, M. D., Yland, J. L. & Rothman, K. J. (2024). "Responding to Reviewers and Editors About Statistical Significance Testing." *Annals of Internal Medicine. American College of Physicians*. p. 1.

programs can be helpful for some participants if not for all,[166] contextual variables, and more.

Here is a succinct statement of the matter,[167] arguing that the p-value,

> should be reported as an exact value and should be regarded as a continuous variable. Consequently, it should be considered fallacious to insert an arbitrary threshold to define results as significant or nonsignificant, as though significant versus nonsignificant results are in some ways categorically different the way people who are dead versus alive are categorically different. Expressed otherwise, declaring statistical significance does not improve our understanding of the data over and above what is already explained by the value of P. In fact, declaring significance may give us a false sense of confidence that a finding exists in the population, while rejecting significance may give us a false sense of confidence that the finding does not exist.

The author goes on to observe that, "[b]asing interpretations on a p-value of 0.05 or other threshold tends to provide an element of certainty to the interpretations. But this certainty is illusory because probability lies along a continuum."[168]

The following issue—the desirability of holding programs constant—is not only a matter of questionable epistemic understanding,

---

[166] Admittedly, when evaluations have large numbers of participants it is possible to disaggregate enrollees into subgroups according to demographic and risk factors, and still obtain statistically significant findings that obtain with some participants but not others. But few indeed are the programs that are large enough to support such analyses so findings that are potentially very meaningful about members of some subgroups likely will be passed over because of how small the subgroups are (and therefore how low the statistical power of the analysis can be).

[167] Andrade, C. (2019). "The P Value and Statistical Significance: Misunderstandings, Explanations, Challenges, and Alternatives." *Indian Journal of Psychological Medicine.* Vol. 41(3) p. 212.

[168] Ibid. p. 213.

it has immediate operational consequences too. Regarding the former, in some ways, it represents a resurrection of Plato's pure, constant, and unchanging forms. On the operational level, it is fraught with difficulties.

The Preference to Hold a Program Static for the Period of the Evaluation

RCTs generally expect that once an evaluation commences the program will keep its elements and processes as constant as humanly possible for the duration of the evaluation.[169] Of course, this is an ideal that, in the hurly-burly of daily life, rarely is reached. But, as program operators have told me in the course of my work, attempting to comply with this "evaluation requirement" puts a considerable strain on front-line staff and their managers who are cautioned that programmatic adjustments in the course of an evaluation can undercut the validity of the study.

But this is more than just an unrealistic and arguably at times an unethical requirement.[170] Among other things, it either suppresses or puts pressure on program operators to ignore emergent issues. Thus, as staff and management learn from their day-to-day work, and see how making adjustments to a program might well improve it and enhance the experience for participants, the evaluator will urge that such adjustments be postponed until the evaluation is finished.[171] But that can be a matter of years—and likely means that

---

[169] Julnes, G., Mark, M., & Shipman, S. (2022). "Conditions to Consider in the Use of Randomized Experimental Designs in Evaluation." *Journal of MultiDisciplinary Evaluation*, 18(42). https://doi.org/10.56645/jmde.v18i42.741.

[170] It is surely worth reminding ourselves that in medical drug trials where early evidence is overwhelmingly positive, the trial will be cut short to bring the drug to market. Similarly, if negatives such as threats to health emerge to a worrisome degree, the trial will be terminated due to the risk it creates for the participants. Why should social program evaluations be any different?

[171] I have observed this happening on more than one occasion.

the results of the evaluation will be out of date the moment it is over and before the results are published.

Evaluators often justify their wish to hold program variables constant during an evaluation by noting, inarguably, that new and thus unevaluated program changes might actually be ineffective at best; maladaptive at worst. So that staff who want to make them are encouraged not to do so because, as far as can be known, that by holding the program "as is" they are not depriving participants of what can be *known* to be service improvement. And making program changes during the evaluation most likely will, however, skew the findings in unpredictable directions.

But we should also remember that it is practitioners who in their daily work translate evaluation findings into applicable knowledge based on their professional experiences. So evaluators should be open to adjusting an evaluation where some aspects of the program in question seem, to staff, in need of change or improvement based on emerging program-generated, practice-based knowledge. And indeed, it must be acknowledged, there are instances where programs do make adjustments to their activities while being evaluated.[172] That's why I referred to the "preference" to hold an RCT evaluation static rather than saying that this is a "requirement." But it would be misleading not to point out that tensions around this matter are real and, at least from what I have observed, can and do emerge in some evaluations.

The fact that RCT methods tend to depend (at least conceptually) on a static description of programs is, I would emphasize, inherently a distortion of reality. If nothing else, we know that the world is in flux, that change is constant. So too with programs even when there are efforts to eliminate changes, especially the subtle fluctuations in their

---

[172] Gordon Berlin emphasized this point to me in a personal correspondence (2024).

day-to-day flow. As the philosopher Alfred North Whitehead argued more specifically,[173] the world, at all levels from the sub-atomic to the human and beyond, consists of relationships among processes. And it takes little reflection to realize that programs and their elements consist entirely of processes manifested in fluid relationships among human beings: front-line staff with program participants, program participants with each other, front-line staff with each other, front-line staff with their supervisors and managers, managers with each other and with executive leadership, executive leadership with boards of directors, leaders with funders, and all of these with the people who constitute the environments in which they live. All of which brings into question what it means to say that a program looked at statically is or isn't effective, does or doesn't work.

To be fair, evaluators are not blind to these matters. They also pay a great deal of attention to program implementation—there is an impressively large research literature devoted exclusively to problems in implementation and how these are addressed, especially when there is the challenge of replicating a given program at new sites with fidelity to the original model.[174] And, of course, some RCTs use "mixed methods"—that is, in addition to the quantitative RCT they also study qualitative phenomena (such as participant attitudes and values and also their feelings about the program itself) to supplement the quantitative data. Some may even use mixed methods to explore some contextual issues that could have a bearing on program effects. Which raises related questions: "How generalizable are RCT findings?" and "How well would a program that had good RCT results in one place do when replicated somewhere else?"

---

[173] Whitehead, A. N. (1933). *Adventures of Ideas*. Simon & Schuster; 1967 edition, The Free Press.

[174] Fixsen, D. L., Naoom, S. F., Blase, K. A., Friedman, R. M. & Wallace, F. (2005). *Implementation Research: A Synthesis of the Literature*. University of South Florida.

The Matters of Generalizability and Replication

While there are good reasons why warehouses of information about program evaluations rely heavily on an evaluative standard that favors RCTs, the reports found there frequently are (mis)used to make dispositive decisions about whether to replicate programs in new sites. This is rather unwise because nothing about RCT methods answers the question of whether a program that has "proven" impacts is generalizable to new contexts. Context is extremely influential when looking at how programs are designed and implemented, and how effective they are. A program that is highly effective in one context may be considerably less (or more) effective in another. This has been seen repeatedly when efforts to replicate programs in new places have been evaluated and found wanting.[175, 176]

RCTs try to deal with this matter by managing down the significance of context through the concept of "treatment as usual" (TAU) to describe what happens in the control group. Since randomization makes the TAU equally probable for both control group members and program participants (before they are enrolled in a program), the thought is that the only difference between what happens to members of the two groups is the program itself and therefore differences in outcomes can be attributed to program effects.[177] But program contexts can both promote and hinder the achievement of outcomes as is illustrated, for example, when multi-systemic family therapy was introduced in Denmark

---

[175] Sundell, K., Ferrer-Wreder, L., & Fraser, M. (2013). "Going Global: A Model for Evaluating Empirically Supported Family-Based Interventions in New Contexts." *Evaluation and the Health Professions*. Vol. 37(2). Sage.

[176] Befani, B. (2012). Op. cit.

[177] Andrée Löfholm, C., Brännström L., Olsson M., & Hansson K. (2013). "Treatment-as-usual in effectiveness studies: What is it and does it matter?" *International Journal of Social Welfare*. Vol. 22. pp. 25–34.

and its effects there were markedly lower than the original evaluation in the U.S. had shown.[178]

Actually, it is well known that numerous so-called "evidence-based" programs with strong impacts that were established by RCT evaluations at their original site have a history of performing disappointingly when replicated. A brief by the U.S. Department of Health and Services[179] identifies three key contextual variables that often are at play, resulting in diminished program effectiveness at replication sites: (a) different motivation of the staff to adopt new programming; (b) different general organizational capacities, and (c) different intervention-specific capacities.

Consider the case of the Center for Employment Training, originally located in San Jose, CA. It trains young people in transitional employment settings and places them with partnering businesses, and it

> ...had shown great promise in the 1980s with large positive effects on their employment and earnings.... Based on these earlier results, the U.S. Department of Labor launched the evaluation of the Center for Employment Training Replication Sites in the mid-1990s, which was designed to test whether the CET model could be implemented successfully in different settings and have similarly positive effects on the youth served. This final report on the evaluation summarizes the replication effort's success and effects on youth after four and a half years. It shows that, even in the sites that best implemented the model, CET had no overall employment and earnings effects for

---

[178] I had this fact brought to my attention on several occasions over the past 20 years when I was consulting to various ministries and agencies in that country.

[179] Dymnicki, A., Wandersman, A., Osher, D., Grigorescu, V., and Huang, L. (2014). *Willing, Able -> Ready: Basics and Policy Implications of Readiness as a Key Component for Implementation of Evidence-Based Interventions*. Office of the Assistant Secretary of Planning and Evaluation, Office of Human Services Policy, U.S. Department of Health and Human Services.

youth in the program, even though it increased partici-pants' hours of training and receipt of credentials.[180, 181]

A very useful article about replication discusses the need to con-duct both an implementation evaluation and an impact evaluation before it is meaningful to consider this option, then lists key points that should be known before the decision is made to replicate.[182] These include (1) that the program was implemented as designed; (2) whether it was effective in producing participant outcomes as intended; (3) an understanding of why the program was effective; (4) clear information about how those program elements that con-tributed to its effectiveness can be implemented in new settings; and (5) whether the program's evaluation showed large enough effects that they would likely be manifested in new contextual conditions. As will have become clear from the foregoing discussion, of these elements item (3) cannot be addressed by an RCT, and even an im-plementation evaluation might well not illuminate this issue if it is conducted within a positivist framework.

So, while RCT results often are generalized to justify program replication plans, there is also the recognition that to do so validly would require (in the words of the harsh RCT critics Ray Pawson

---

[180] Miller, C., Bos, J. M., Porter, K. E., Tseng, F. M., & Abe, Y. (2005). *The Challenge of Repeating Success in a Changing World: Final Report on the Center for Employment Training Replication Sites*. MDRC:xi.

[181] Gordon Berlin commented to me in a 2022 personal communication that "the findings do raise questions about whether a dynamic program like CET can, in fact, be replicated. CET-San Jose is unique in so many ways, having grown organically over 20 years, with an unusually committed founder and staff, very strong ties to the local community, and a tradition of political advocacy on behalf of the local Hispanic community. Perhaps a homegrown model like CET cannot be easily export-ed in a top-down way to other areas. More research is needed on how to transfer promising models to other areas, particularly given the difficulties that at-risk youth face in today's competitive job market."

[182] Harris, A. (2010). "Six Steps to Successfully Scale Impact in the Nonprofit Sector." *The Evaluation Exchange*. Harvard Family Research Project, vol, XV(1) p. 4.

and Nick Tilley) that one "control every single potentially confounding influence."[183] But perhaps we need not take the argument this far. A very useful discussion of the generalizability of so-called "evidence-supported interventions" (ESIs) notes that "[At] least four explanations appear plausible for the mixed results in replication trials. One has to do with methodological differences across trials. A second deals with ambiguities in the cultural adaptation process. A third explanation is that ESIs in failed replications have not been adequately implemented. A fourth source of variation derives from unanticipated contextual influences that might affect the results of ESIs when transported to other cultures and countries."[184] Steffen Bohni Nielsen, a well-regarded Danish evaluator, in considering this issue notes that "[t]here is a whole literature on the issue of generalization. If one—deductively—can infer the findings to be true for an entire population sharing similar characteristics, programs ought to be replicable and transferable. *They seldom are*"[185] (emphasis added).

Summary Reflection on RCTs

The most fundamental epistemic point regarding RCTs is that contrary to what many people believe, RCTs cannot ultimately "prove" nor "disprove" a program's effectiveness. Rather, they serve the rhetorical function of producing credible evidence by asserting "objectivity" within the positivist worldview that is hegemonic in our society. Furthermore, while it is fair to say that RCTs are the most elegant and even the most likely evaluation method at our disposal when the concern is to limit

---

[183] Pawson, R. and Tilley, N, (1997). Op. cit. p. 118.

[184] Sundell, K., Ferrer-Wreder, L., & Fraser, M. (2013). Op.cit.

[185] Steffen Bohni Nielsen made this point in a personal communication with me in June 2023.

the influences of some important sources of research biases, they do so in reductive ways that ultimately limit what we can learn about how and why programs work, for whom they are best suited, and in what contexts they are most effective.[186]

Nevertheless, RCTs do make fundamental contributions in our quest to learn about social programs and what they can—and can't— accomplish. True, individual RCTs cannot provide the full range of information needed to make responsible decisions such as whether to fund or replicate programs. But *they are an essential first step* in developing the kind of dependable knowledge we need to design, implement, manage, and (in some cases) replicate social programs.[187] And this, of course, is a social imperative.

At this point, I want to emphasize that I don't intend my critique of RCTs to promote the nihilistic view that rigorous evaluations aren't important, nor that the views of practitioners and program participants alone suffice as sources of information to assess the effectiveness of programs in producing valuable outcomes. Nor am I even remotely suggesting that it is sufficient for programs or their evaluators to collect outcome data alone, that doing so is just as informative as RCTs. Any evaluation that is trying to determine the usefulness of a program for its participants simply has to go beyond that. Specifically, if outcomes are to have much meaning they must be collected, analyzed, and understood through comparison with other rigorously collected data.

---

[186] It is worth reminding ourselves that the data produced by RCTs are averages of change(s) for both the participant and the control groups. In effect, program effectiveness means that the distribution of results for individuals in the program group has been shifted toward the intended end of the distribution curve, either by pushing the bottom end toward the intended end or by shifting the whole distribution in that direction. Results for individuals are in the raw data that rarely if ever are reported publicly.

[187] Here again I thank Gordon Berlin for emphasizing this point to me.

Why? As was discussed in Chapter VI with regard to Michael Scriven's proposal for a "goals-free" evaluation method, if one simply collects data on a bunch of outcomes there is no way to determine whether nor to what degree the findings are "false positives," "false negatives"—or even a mix of both.

However, there isn't one "best" relationship in terms of which outcomes can be compared to other kinds of information. Certainly, the use of a counterfactual in the manner of RCTs is a strong option. But there are other meaningful frameworks, alternative sets of data against which to examine program outcomes. One example is provided by so-called "realist evaluations" where the nuanced interrelations of a program's context(s), change mechanisms, and outcomes are studied in great detail and successive iterations; it is for this reason that realist evaluations are discussed in considerable detail in Chapter X and beyond.

My hope is that creating a kind of dialogue between these two evaluation methods will afford readers an opportunity to join in the discussion and through it to explore and refine their beliefs and assumptions about evaluation methods, evaluative questions to ask, and ultimately about what kind of knowledge evaluations can yield.

A final thought: It's about more than RCTs. In general, we should be careful about uncritically adopting positivist thinking. Period. In discussing these matters Hermann Weyl, a highly regarded philosopher and mathematician, used the example of a house: "The positivists try to nail a roof on by excluding the open sky which they do not see; that is blindness."[188]

---

[188] Weyl, H. (2009). *Mind and Nature*. Princeton University Press. p. 192.

Chapter IX

ESSENTIALISM OPERATIONALIZED: CONSTRUCTIVIST AND REALIST EVALUATIONS

As discussed in Chapter V, essentialism is inherently an idealist approach to understanding the world. In the area of program evaluations, one important essentialist approach is *constructivist evaluation*. This approach emerged with a high degree of intentionality in opposition to the instrumentalist positivism of RCTs. Of all idealist approaches to program evaluation, I find constructivism to be the most fully realized in that it has well-defined methods (something realist evaluation has yet to achieve, as will be seen below).

Constructivist Epistemology

Like all brands of idealist thinking, constructivism holds that all "reality" is a human creation. Thus social reality too is a human artifact, a product of our minds built by moving past our individual subjective experiences to reach agreements with others through aggregated, iterative feedback loops. These agreements then become determinative social constructs or structures and thus are organizers of human thoughts and behaviors (e.g., when administrative policies are adopted, family values are enunciated over dinner, children are rewarded or reprimanded, war is declared, a run on banks emerges seemingly without cause, fake news is treated as true, and so on).[189] As one author puts it, "the social construction of reality is pervasive."[190]

John Searle, a leading constructivist philosopher, grounds his thinking very specifically in the function of language in human affairs. Using the term "social ontology" to denote the nature of the world as an artifact of our collective minds, he states flatly that there is one and only one mechanism for this to happen. That mechanism is linguistic and "we apply it over and over with different contents,"[191] thereby bringing everything about the world as we know it into focus. "Social reality," he says, "has a formal structure as simple and elegant as the structure of the language used to create it."[192] For Searle, reality—specifically society and its institutions—is entirely subjective, not in any way objectively "true." As he sees it, to understand this social ontology one must, perforce, understand the subjectivity of individuals.

Constructivism—The Most Fully Realized Idealist Approach to Program Evaluation

Constructivist evaluations evolved from that branch of cultural anthropology which emphasizes the symbolic nature of culture and the ways in which people belonging to a given culture develop shared understandings of the world.[193] Ethnography, at least to the extent that it has remained predominantly inductive

---

[189] Berger, P. L. and Luckmann, T. (1967). *The Social Construction of Reality*. Doubleday Anchor.

[190] Ross, J. (2008). *Thought and World: The Hidden Necessities*. University of Notre Dame Press. p. 166.

[191] Searle, J. R. (2010). *Making the Social World: The Structure of Human Civilization*. Oxford University Press. p. 7.

[192] Ibid. p. 16

[193] Geertz, C. (1973). *The Interpretation of Cultures*. Basic Books.

in its methods, has been largely interpretive and comparative rather than experimental in its orientation.[194] It is an approach to learning about and seeking to understand things using methods that are grounded directly in the researcher's experiences rather than on data generated by mechanistic processes meeting statistical requirements.[195]

Unlike RCTs, constructivist evaluations do not start with predetermined categories and indicators in terms of which data will be collected and organized. Rather, they develop these categories inductively and do so iteratively in the course of ongoing data collection and analysis. In that sense, rather than prescribing the data that must be obtained, analytical categories are developed in response to emerging patterns in the data as they are collected.[196]

> A central function of this approach is to forestall researchers from grasping too quickly on a theory—that is, the set of ideas designed to explain the phenomenon under study... researchers continue to evolve the theory in relation to continued observation until they are confident that the theory holds and can provide a useful answer to the research question.[197]

What sometimes is called *grounded constructivist research* generally works as follows: First, data of likely interest are collected. Then the data are organized into intuitively meaningful units that are named and then compared with each other. Based on observed

---

[194] Geertz, C. (1983). Local Knowledge. *Further Essays in Interpretive Anthropology.* Basic Books.

[195] Hunter, D. E. & Whitten, P. (1976). *The Study of Cultural Anthropology.* Harper and Row. pp. 112-18.

[196] Glaser, B. G. & Strauss, A. L. (1967). *The Discovery of Grounded Theory: Strategies for Qualitative Research.* Aldine. pp. 5-6.

[197] (2021). Critical-Constructivist Grounded Theory Research. The American Psychological Association.

patterns the units are organized into categories, which then are combined with each other into higher order categories. This process continues until the researchers can construct a robust hierarchy of categories, with the category emerging at the top expressing the analytically constructed theory that (tentatively) explains the data—or at least describes the specific data set. This "gives researchers confidence in describing how their central findings emerged because they can point to the categories beneath them that led to their composition."[198] When applied to program evaluations this approach provides an easy-to-understand logic in terms of which the findings can be seen as plausible. Which is as much as one could hope for.[199]

The chasm separating the epistemologies of idealism and materialism is profound. But is it fundamentally unbridgeable? Let's consider realism, an epistemic framework that, as we discussed in Chapter II, seems to offer a possible bridge between the two. An inquiry into realist evaluation methods will provide us with the means to do so.

Realist Program Evaluation

Realist evaluation was launched with something of a roar in 1997 by the British evaluators Ray Pawson and Nick Tilley when they published their book *Realistic Evaluation*.[200] They suggested that evaluation is at a "watershed," by which they meant to say that the field is a ubiquitous, "sweepingly successful social movement" that is valued and used as a way of justifying decisions in universalist

---

[198] Ibid. pp. 7-8.

[199] Guba, Y. & Lincoln, E. (1989). Effective Evaluation: Improving the Usefulness of Evaluation Results Through Responsive and Naturalistic Approaches. Jossey-Bass.

[200] Pawson, R. & Tilley, N. (1997). Op.cit.

terms. On the other hand, they observe, that we are "living in an age of cynicism and cultural relativism" where human understanding is perceived to be "locked into the particular discourse which surrounds each social group." They seek to escape the horns of this dilemma by arguing for a new approach to evaluation that they call "realistic evaluation," by which they mean evaluation that (1) "deals with the real"; (2) uses "*realist* methodology"; and (3) is "*realistic*."[201] Basing their approach on the study of causes and effects in social programs, they adopt the epistemology of realism and its application to scientific methods.[202] They state flatly: "To be realistic is to acknowledge that there is no universal 'logic of evaluation', no absolute 'science of valuing', no general 'warrant for decision making' applicable to all subjects."[203] To put a fine point on it, the authors are, without any inhibitions, launching a frontal attack on positivism in general and RCTs in particular.

Now commonly referred to as *realist evaluation*, this approach has its roots in *theory-driven evaluation*, which arose as a counterforce to the original "black box" positivism of RCTs and related evaluation methods. We can trace this to 1981 with the publication of a seminal article by Huey-Tsyh Chen and Peter H. Rossi,[204] which then was elaborated upon notably by Chen[205] and Carol Weiss.[206] Theory-driven evaluation insists on the importance of unpacking a program's "black box," of looking inside the program, of effectively

---

[201] Ibid. pp. xi-xiii. (emphases in original).

[202] Bhaskar, R. (1975). *A Realist Theory of Science*. Harvester Press.

[203] Ibid. p xiii.

[204] Chen H.-T. and Rossi, P. H. (1981). "The multi-goal theory-driven approach to evaluation: A model linking basic and applied social science." In Freedman, H. and Soloman, M. (Eds.) Evaluation Studies Review Annual. Vol. 6. Sage. pp 38-54.

[205] Chen, H.-T. (1990). *Theory-driven evaluations*. Sage.

[206] Weiss, C. H. (1972). *Evaluation*. Prentice Hall.

making its sides transparent. Theory-driven evaluations are intended to explore and investigate the essences of programs (see Chapter V), and thereby come to understand them. Among other things, this gives practitioners information they can use to make needed adjustments to improve their programs—to utilize evaluations to enhance their contributions to the social good.[207]

As has been noted previously, realist evaluation has not caught on in the United States.[208] For the very reasons that have sold Americans on the positivist, quantified results of RCTs, considering realist evaluations as a legitimate alternative to RCTs is almost anathema. Among other things, this is because realist evaluation methods reject "the positivist notion that interventions in and of themselves cause outcomes,"[209] insisting on a much more complex set of cause-and-effect assumptions that we will look at shortly. Furthermore, realist evaluations tend to be strongly qualitative in emphasis; this fits poorly with the strong bias in the U.S. toward a quantitatively renderable, positivist worldview—and therefore leaves realist evaluations in a relatively weak position with regard to their credibility in this country. Thus they remain, at least for the time being, in want of rhetorical validity in the context of American culture (see Chapter V). However, realist evaluations are in full swing around the world, so it is time for us to look at them more closely.

---

[207] Patton, M. Q. (2008). Op. cit.

[208] I am grateful to Stephen Bohni Nielsen, Director General of the Danish National Research Center for the Working Environment, for bringing realist evaluations to my attention.

[209] Greenhalgh T., Greenhalg, J., Pawson R., Manzano, A., Wong G., Jagosh, J. & Westhorp, G. (2016). "Quality standards for realist evaluation. For evaluators and peer-reviewers." *The RAMESES II Project.* Available at: http://ramesesproject.org/media/RE_Quality_Standards_for_evaluators_and_peer_reviewers.pdf.

Chapter X

REALIST EVALUATION METHODS

The key requirement of realist evaluations is that to be assessed usefully, a program has to have a well-articulated "theory of change" laying out its basic logic, its cause and effect assumptions. But such a theory should not be framed solely in terms of the easily seen and quantified elements of positivist evaluations such as RCTs. Rather, they should look for the hard to see (if not invisible) aspects of programs and their contexts, just as the expanded world view of realism would suggest (see Chapter II). In particular, realist evaluators emphasize that it is essential to specify the underlying **mechanisms** by which desired changes are to be produced. These can then be tested by an appropriate evaluation design.[210]

But first a warning of sorts. It is essential to recognize that *realist evaluations, like the programs this approach is used to evaluate, must be understood as sets of theories.* What follows will illuminate this perhaps puzzling statement.

---

[210] Chen, H.-T. (1990). Op. cit.

Realist Evaluations and Their Project
to Develop Methodological Standards

While as of yet, there are no generally accepted standards[211] for realist data collection methods nor for their data analyses,[212] the goals of realist evaluation are clear. As discussed above, with programs that are complex in their design and implementation, and for understanding often complex contextual influences on program results, RCTs tend to be insufficient.[213] Recognizing this, about a decade ago realist evaluators began to develop guidelines for conducting their evaluations.

> A relatively new approach…to addressing these problems is realist evaluation. A form of theory-driven evaluation, based on realist philosophy…it aims to advance understanding of why these complex interventions work, how, for whom, in what context and to what extent—and also to explain the many situations in which a programme fails to achieve the anticipated benefit. Realist evaluation assumes both that social systems and structures are 'real' (because they have real effects) and also that human actors respond differently to interventions in different circumstances. To understand how an intervention might generate different outcomes in different circumstances, realism introduces the concept of mechanisms—underlying changes in the reasoning and behaviour of participants that are triggered in particular contexts. For

---

[211] However, initial efforts to develop such standards are underway but have yet to be institutionalized within the realist evaluation community the way quality standards have been among RCT evaluators. See: Greenhalgh T., Wong G., Jagosh J., et al. (2015). "Protocol—the RAMESES II study: developing guidance and reporting standards for realist evaluation." *BMJ Open* 5:e008567.

[212] I had this conclusion confirmed by the Danish evaluator Steffen Bohni Nielsen in a personal communication; February 2024. He has published extensively on the theory and methods of realist evaluations.

[213] Craig, P. Dieppe, P., Macintyre, S., Michie, S., Nazareth, I. & Pettigrew, M. (2006). Developing and evaluating complex interventions: new guidance. Medical Research Council.

example, a school-based feeding programme may work by short-term hunger relief in young children in a low-income rural setting where famine has produced overt nutritional deficiencies, but for teenagers in a troubled inner-city community where many young people are disaffected, it may work chiefly by making pupils feel valued and nurtured.[214]

The authors go on to observe: "Since programmes work differently in different contexts and through different change mechanisms, programmes cannot simply be replicated from one context to another and automatically achieve the same outcomes. Theory-based *understandings* about 'what works for whom, in what contexts, and how' are, however, transferable"[215] (emphasis added).

The Tenuous Epistemic Status of Realist Evaluations

Stepping back for a moment, it must be understood that the launch of realist evaluations by Pawson and Tilley in 1997[216] was an explosive event. In a paradigm-shattering break with positivism, *realist evaluations conceive of programs as social systems embedded in other social systems; these operate in terms of organized groupings of theories (ideas), rather than as purely physical entities with discrete boundaries.* In fact, realist evaluations have been called "theories incarnate." They require program theories to go beyond the usual (positivist) logic models that describe simple (and quantifiable) series of inputs, outputs, and outcomes. "Program theory goes a step further and attempts to build an explanatory account of how the program works, with whom, and under what circumstances"[217]

---

[214] Greenhalgh T., Greenhalg, J., Pawson R., et al. (2016). Op. cit. p. 2.

[215] Greenhalgh T., Wong G., Jagosh J., et al. (2016). Ibid. p. 2.

[216] Pawson, R. & Tilley, N. (1997). Op. cit.

[217] Asbury, B. & Leeuw, F. L. (2010). "Unpacking Black Boxes: Mechanisms and Theory Building in Education." *American Journal of Evaluation* 31(3):363-381.

(emphasis in original). These central questions of realist evaluations stand in sharp contrast to the much more limited and limiting RCT questions of whether and to what degree a given program "works."

Realist evaluations are theories about how to understand the theories that constitute the programs they are evaluating. They see programs not as lapidary entities, but rather as theoretical (idealist) constructs that are designed and implemented in ways that are open systems embedded in wider social systems, that are experienced in different ways by various stakeholders (including the program's participants) and that depend highly on, and vary with, inherently shifting contextual considerations. They are grounded in an appreciation that while there may be something in the material world that we choose to call a program, there is far more going on in and around any program than an evaluator ever will be able to observe or measure. Therefore, far from describing a "reality" that is somehow out there and apart from us, realist program evaluations do not aspire to prove (or disprove) claims about a program's impacts. Instead, *they produce testable theories about what a program's mechanisms for producing change consist of, whom the program is serving, what outcomes it may be achieving, and what influences contextual factors may exert.*[218] In a nutshell, *realist evaluations aim to understand programs*, not to explain them in reductive, positivist terms. And being intentionally iterative, realist evaluations build in a series of multiple testings of their findings about a given program's effectiveness.

Here, repeated a bit differently, is what realist evaluations are and what they do. Since from a realist perspective programs are seen

---

[218] Pawson, R. & Tilley, N. (2005). "Realistic Evaluation" in Mathison, S. (Ed.), *Encyclopedia of Evaluation*. Sage. pp. 362-367.

as sets of theories, realist evaluators develop relevant theories about a program, then formulate key hypotheses regarding the interplay of program context(s), mechanisms for producing intended changes, and program outcomes. Then they test each hypothesis separately. "This means collecting data, not just about programme impacts or the processes of programme implementation, but about the specific aspects of programme context that might impact on programme outcomes and about the specific mechanisms that might be creating change."[219] The results of the first analyses of the interrelations among context, mechanism, and outcomes then become the source of new, more refined hypotheses. In turn, these will be tested and the process will be repeated in a series of iterations where at each stage of the progression the findings are analyzed and refined. How often and how many times does this need to be done? There are no standards for this process, so in the end common sense has to prevail and the progression will be halted once it does not seem that further iterations will add value and the conclusions meet the needs of key program stakeholders.

It will have become obvious from the preceding description that *realist evaluations are case studies of programs.* They do not depend on the experimental method to shed light on causality; rather, *they are grounded in observation and the inductive method* for extracting meaning from emerging patterns of data. In this, they resemble the classical approach of anthropology where participant observers witness what is happening around them and interview the people in whom they are interested to discover their understanding of things.[220] This is an iterative process that requires the interlacing

---

[219] Greenhalgh T, Wong G., & Jagosh J., et al. (2015). Op. cit. p. 2.

[220] De Waal Malefijt, A. (1974). Images of Man. Alfred A. Knopf; Geertz, C. (1973). The Interpretation of Cultures. Basic Books; Hunter, D. E. & Whitten, P. (1976). The Study of Anthropology. Harper & Row. (cf. especially Ch. 2).

of data collection and concurrent data analysis.[221] And perhaps it is worth mentioning that Michael Scriven, the "father" of program RCTs, in fact, appreciated that the case study method is "recognized as capable in principle of extended causal analysis"[222] and cites what is called the "success case method."[223]

Pawson and Tilley[224] proffer the basic assumptions that underly this method, which can be summarized as follows:

o In their effort to address important social issues, programs work (that is, produce outcomes) by enabling participants to make new kinds of choices by changing their reasoning as well as the resources they have at their disposal;

o The combination of reasoning and resources are the mechanisms through which programs work to produce outcomes (or may not, as the case may be);

o Such mechanisms, however, may work differently for different people, in part because the context(s) of a program may affect participants differentially;

o Consequently, a program's context(s) make a difference in the outcomes they achieve (promoting some, inhibiting others). Indeed, it is the interaction of contexts and mechanisms that produce program outcomes or impacts in an individualized way for program participants.

---

[221] Nielsen, S. B. & Lemire, S. (n.d.). "Nothing as Practical as an Analytical Strategy in Realist Evaluation: Findings and Recommendations From a Comprehensive Review."

[222] Scriven, M. (2005). "Causation." In Mathison, S. (Ed.) *Encyclopedia of Evaluation*. Sage. pp. 43-47.

[223] Brinkerhoff, R. O. (2003). *The Success Case Method*. Berrett-Koehler.

[224] Pawson R. & Tilley N. (1997). Op. cit.

Rules for Realist Evaluations

Pawson and Tilley propose seven "rules"—or, perhaps more accurately, concepts—for conducting realist evaluations[225]:

1. *Generative causation*: Evaluators need to attend to how and why social programs have the potential to cause change.

2. *Ontological depth*: Evaluators need to penetrate beneath the surface of the observable inputs and outputs of a program.

3. *Mechanisms*: Evaluators need to focus on how the causal mechanisms that generate social and behavioural problems are removed or countered through the alternative causal mechanisms introduced in a social program.

4. *Contexts*: Evaluators need to understand the contexts within which program mechanisms can be activated successfully.

5. *Outcomes*: Evaluators need to understand what the outcomes of a program are and how they are produced.

6. *CMO configurations*: In order to develop transferable and cumulative lessons from research, evaluators need to orient their thinking to context-mechanism-outcome pattern configurations.

7. *Teacher-learner processes*: In order to construct and test context-mechanism-outcome explanations, evaluators need to engage in a teacher-learner relationship with program policymakers, practitioners, and participants.

---

[225] Pawson, R. and Tilley, N. (1997). Op. cit. pp. 215-219.

The Realist CMO Configuration

All of which brings us to the configurational formula of realist evaluation:

Context + *Mechanism* = *Outcome*.

Context in Realist Evaluations

Pawson and Tilley broach the subject of context compellingly enough that they are worth quoting in full:

> All social programs wrestle with prevailing contextual conditions. Programs are always introduced *into* pre-existing social contexts and…these prevailing social conditions are of crucial importance when it comes to explaining the successes and failures of social programs. By social context, we do not refer simply to the spacial or geographical or institutional location into which programs are embedded…it is the prior set of social rules, norms, values and interrelationships gathered in these places which sets limits on the efficacy of program mechanisms[226] (emphasis in original).

So for realist evaluations context is treated differently than it is in RCT evaluations. Rather than treating program contexts as a fact of life that has to be *managed* via a counterfactual, for realist evaluators program contexts need to be *understood* because they interact causally with program mechanisms. This means, among other things, that program outcomes are always to be thought of as emergent phenomena that inevitably are in flux (as Heraclitus would insist)—a very different way of thinking about things than the more statically conceived, quantified impacts that RCTs identify.

Pawson and Tilley go on to argue that a great shortcoming of positivist evaluations is exactly with regard to the matter of context:

---

[226] Pawson, R. & Tilley, N. (1997). Op. cit. p. 70.

"It is…futile for researchers to ignore and anonymize the contexts of their programs as in experimental evaluation [i.e., RCTs] and we have no hesitation in pointing to this lack of attention to the social conditions which pre-exist and endure through programs as one of the great omissions of evaluation research."[227]

Consider, for example, the case of **Roca, Inc.,**[228] whose mission is "to be a relentless force in disrupting incarceration, poverty, and racism by engaging the young adults, police, and systems at the center of urban violence in relationships to address trauma, find hope, and drive change." Roca currently operates in Chelsea, MA; the greater Boston area; Springfield, MA; Baltimore, MD; and Hartford, CT. It works with young adults who are at the highest levels of risk of being perpetrators or victims of street violence, including shootings.[229] In their words: "Roca finds and focuses only on young people at the center of urban violence— those who are traumatized, full of distrust, and are trapped in a cycle of violence and poverty that traditional youth programs alone can't break."

Roca's program has undergone several evaluations. One, a benchmarking study by Abt Associates,[230] showed that ifrom 2018–2021, of the young people served "85% did not recidivate within one year of enrollment, 76% did not recidivate within two years, and 70% did not recidivate within three years. This is a 42%-46% reduction

---

[227] Ibid.

[228] This discussion is based on the materials available on the Roca website, access at: https://rocainc.org/.

[229] I have consulted to Roca a half-dozen times over the past 20 years, mostly working with them on iterations of their theory of change.

[230] Abt Associates (2021). "Roca's Impact: An Update on External Evaluation Results." Access at: n https://rocainc.org/wp-content/uploads/2021/09/Roca-Evaluation-Update%5EJ-September-2021.pdf).

in recidivism when compared to a similar group analyzed by the Council on State Governments [which]… recently reported three-year re-incarceration rates of 52% and 56% for youth ages 18–24 who were released from Massachusetts county jails and state prisons, respectively."

Roca's program consists of the following elements:[231]

o *Relentless outreach and engagement.* "We find young people at the center of violence and show up at their door—and we keep showing up every day until they open up."

o *Transformational Relationships.* "Youth workers are trained to gain participants' trust, establish meaningful relationships with them, and support them through different stages of the program. They provide intensive case management and are expected to be available 24 hours a day."

o *Cognitive Behavioral Theory*—referred to as rewiring of the brain. In their words, "Trauma keeps young people stuck in survival mode, so they keep repeating the same negative behaviors. Roca's cognitive behavioral theory (Rewire CBT) skills heal trauma by building new neural pathways."[232]

o *Practice relentless patience.* "Relapse is a crucial moment of learning, so we relentlessly support each young person through temporary failures, no matter how many times it takes."

---

[231] Hossain, F. & Wasserman, K. (2021). *Using Cognitive Behavioral Therapy to Address Trauma and Reduce Violence Among Baltimore's Young Men.* MDRC. July.

[232] It is hardly surprising that Roca staff who were more comfortable working with Rewire were better able to implement it than were those who found it challenging. Here too we have a potential mechanism for producing intended outcomes: the level of confidence and competence of staff while they are delivering key activities, which may also be the result of a more basic mechanism, namely staff training.

o *Rewire the system.* "We relentlessly engage a vast array of police and other system partners to test new strategies, share critical information, and coordinate case management to improve outcomes for young people and the whole community."

The last listed element is what we usually think about when considering a program's context—that is, the institutional setting and the surrounding institutional infrastructures (schools, police, courts, etc.). However, a realist evaluation would consider the first three listed items to be contextual elements as well. Furthermore, while a positivist evaluation would certainly take note of the second item (Transformational Relationships) and identify it as a program element, it is unlikely to take note of how individual Roca staff apply it in their various and varying interactions with each young person they serve—that is, the mechanisms of program delivery.

Specifically, Roca recognizes that the condition of the relationship between a young person and a staff member will profoundly affect how the staff member communicates CBT methods and how the young person internalizes them. So, and much to its credit, Roca tracks the developmental stages of these relationships using the transtheoretical stages of development: (1) pre-cognition, (2) thinking or contemplation, (3) planning or preparation, (4) practicing, and (5) maintaining[233]; and staff adjust their application of the CBT methods accordingly. But having reviewed Roca's RCT evaluations to date, I am not aware of any of them discussing the stages of development as a key contextual condition unique to each participant with a specific staff member in

---

[233] Prochaska, J. O. and Velicer, W. F. (1997). "The transtheoretical model of health behavior change. *American Journal of Health Promotion.* Sep-Oct. Vol. 12(1):38-48.

a given moment in time nor as a way of managing the program mechanisms[234] that help Roca's young people learn and change their behavior from participating in the program.

To summarize, for realist evaluations the causal power of a program "lies in its underlying mechanism (M), namely its basic theory about how programme resources will influence the subject's actions. Whether this mechanism is actually triggered depends on context (C), the characteristics of both the subjects and the programme locality. Programmes, especially over the course of a number of trials, will therefore have diverse impacts over a range of effects, a feature known as the outcome pattern (O)."[235]

Mechanisms in Realist Evaluations

In the social sciences, there is a large literature on mechanisms and mechanism-based approaches to theory building. Central to this work is the idea that to understand social phenomena deeply it is essential to identify the mechanisms linking cause and effect relations.[236] Clearly, this includes the evaluation of social programs and the outcomes they produce.

---

[234] Having worked episodically with Roca on their theory of change over close to three decades, I have long held the hypothesis that the most powerful mechanism driving Roca's success with its program participants is that Roca is providing them with what psychotherapists would call a "corrective emotionally experience" where deep relationships are formed between staff and clients in which the young people are accepted without reservation while, simultaneously, staff hold them to high standards. Some would call this a loving relationship, in the best sense of the word. Needless to say, no evaluation of Roca to date has investigated this. See: Bridges, M. R. (2206). "Activating the Corrective Emotional Experience." Journal of Clinical Psychology: In Session. Vol. 62(5):551-568. Wiley.

[235] Pawson, R. (2002). "Evidence-Based policy: The Promise of 'Realist Synthesis'." *Evaluation*. Vol 8(3):157-181. p. 165.

[236] Astbury, B. & Leeuw, F. L. (2010). "Unpacking Black Boxes: Mechanisms and Theory Building in Education." *American Journal of Evaluation* 31(3):363-381.

Realist evaluations focus "not only on outcomes themselves… but also the underlying generative mechanisms that produce the outcomes. *Social programs, then, consist not just of what we observe (i.e., program inputs, activities, and outcomes) but also of interactions between mechanisms and contexts, which account for what we observe*"[237](emphasis added).

It is worth emphasizing that for realist evaluators mechanisms often are hidden. In other words, we cannot rely solely on observation to discover them. Instead, we have to go below empirical, surface-level descriptions to identify the underlying mechanisms that account for patterns of outcomes; these are only likely to be revealed inductively through qualitative inquiries in focus groups, one-on-one interviews, and participatory observations. But of course, mechanisms, though not necessarily observable, can nevertheless exert pressures on peoples' thinking, feeling, and behavior that lead to observable consequences. For example, a famous study called "Pygmalion in the Classroom,"[238] in which at the beginning of the school term teachers were told that a randomly selected group of students was uncommonly gifted, led eight months later to those students having gained much more in terms of measured IQ points than did other students in their class. This is sometimes described as a self-fulfilling prophecy or, in more technical language, a belief-formation mechanism. Such mechanisms, it is safe to say, are at play in schools everywhere and an evaluation would not uncover them unless the researcher was on the lookout for them in the first place.

---

[237] Astbury B. & Leeuw F. L. (2010). Op. cit. pp. 370-371.

[238] Rosenthal, R., & Jacobson, L. (1968). *Pygmalion in the Classroom*. Holt, Rinehart and Winston, Inc.

Importantly, *mechanisms often are very sensitive to variations in context.* Mechanisms discovered in a particular evaluation should not be treated as generalizable constants. Whatever they may consist of in any given instance, they always operate through the behavior of people, and human behavior is very contextualized. Whether or not a particular mechanism is activated depends to a great extent on the people involved—and specifically their thoughts and inclinations. When all is said and done, programs "work" only if and to the extent that people (both program staff and intended beneficiaries) decide to make them work—and are operating in a context that supports their ability to do so.

Consider the following programs: **Roca** in Massachusetts and Hartford, Connecticut; the **Connecticut Violence Intervention Program** in New Haven, **StreetSafe** in Bridgeport, and the **Compass Youth Collaborative** in Hartford; also, **Chicago Cred** in Illinois.[239] They all are working with young people at high risk for committing or becoming victims of violence; and independently they have found that although it is not itself a program element, the building of trust between the youth workers and the young people in their respective programs is a necessary condition—indeed what here is called a context—for creating the conditions under which program participants are open to learning from staff—which in turn engenders desired behavioral outcomes.

A key clarification is needed here: Astbury and Leeuw[240] make a point of emphasizing that evaluators often conflate program mechanisms and program activities. This is a mistake because *mechanisms are what mediate between program activities and the outcomes*

---

[239] These are programs which I have visited and to which, in some cases, I have consulted.

[240] Astbury, B. & Leeuw, F. L. (2010). Op. cit.

that program participants manifest. They can't be discovered quantitatively but rather must be discovered using qualitative research methods. Yet they are the causal means at work that produce program outcomes.[241]

Outcomes in Realist Evaluations

Outcomes in realist evaluations are pretty much the same as outcomes in RCTs: the more or less regular changes in participants' attitudes, knowledge, skills, and behavior. That is, outcomes are the empirical changes in participants that are measurable and recognized and have been produced by causal mechanisms that are triggered in specific contexts.[242]

However, it is worth noting that this (simple) formula has some shortcomings. "For one, the program component is conspicuously absent from the core theoretical structure of the realist inquiry—the context-mechanism-outcome configuration. This absence is, of course, intentional on behalf of Pawson and Tilley; after all, the name of the game for the realist evaluator is exactly to focus and direct attention to the underlying mechanisms of the program (as opposed to the program itself). However, we suspect that the difficulty expressed by some authors in distinguishing between program components and mechanisms stems, at least in part, from the lack of explicit identification of program components in the CMO template."[243]

---

[241] Hedström, P. & Swedberg, R. (Eds.). (1998). *Social Mechanisms: An analytical approach to social theory.* Cambridge University Press.

[242] Lemire, S., Kwako, A., Nielsen, S. B., Christie, C. A., Donaldson, S. I., & Leeuw, F. L. (2020). "What is this thing called a mechanism? Findings from a review of realist evaluations." In Schmitt, J. (Ed.). *Causal Mechanisms in Program Evaluation.* New Directions for Evaluation, 16: 73–86.

[243] Lemire, S., Kwako, A., Nielsen, S. B., Christie, C. A., Donaldson, S. I., & Leeuw, F. L. (2020). Ibid. pp. 73–86.

Chapter XI

HOW REALIST EVALUATIONS DEAL WITH CAUSALITY

As was mentioned above, a useful article describes four major approaches to causality.[244] RCTs use counterfactual and probabilistic approaches. Realist evaluations, in contrast, rely on *generative* and *configurational* approaches.

The Generative Approach to Causation

By the term *generative causation* realist evaluators mean the chain of cause and effect events in which mechanisms of change, brought to bear by an intervention (program) in a series of contexts, and repeatedly over time, engender certain outcomes in specific individuals.[245] As mentioned earlier, it is an inductive approach that sees programs not as enduring constellations of activities, but rather as iterative chains of cause and effect. And in this perspective, *programs consist of theories and hypotheses put into action within a given social system and tested over time* through repeated data collection and analyses that, as contexts change, produce new

---

[244] Palenberg, M. A. (2023). Op.cit.

[245] Mayne , J. (1999). *Addressing attribution through contribution analysis: Using performance measures sensibly*. Discussion paper. Office of the Auditor General of Canada.

theories and new hypotheses.[246] Generative causation, then, is not to be conceived of as an event external to program participants. As Pawson and Tilley put it,

> The change generated by social interventions should be viewed 'internally' and takes the form of the release of underlying causal powers of individuals and communities. Realists do not conceive that programs 'work', rather it is the actions of stakeholders that makes them work, and the causal potential of an initiative takes the form of providing reasons and resources to enable program participants to change.[247]

They go on to state that "The evaluator needs to understand the conditions required for the program's causal potential to be released and whether this has been released in practice."[248] Thus, in realist evaluations the task at hand is not to demonstrate (nor even to hypothesize) "the conjunction whereby program X produces outcome Y."[249] Rather, the task is to uncover how, iteratively and in specific contexts, mechanisms influence program participants to think differently and change their behaviors. And this, in fact, also summarizes the configurational approach to causation.

The Configurational Approach to Causation

This approach involves looking beyond the net effects of a program to relational considerations—i.e., the *Context + Mechanism = Outcome* configurational formula. As mentioned above, such configurations display the multiple ways that causal conditions

---

[246] Mayne, .J (2019). "Assessing the relative importance of causal factors." *CDI Practice Paper 21*. Centre for Development Impact.

[247] Pawson, R. & Tilley, K. (1997). Op. cit. p. 215.

[248] Ibid.

[249] Ibid.

may work together to produce outcomes. "Configurational theorising revolves around three tenets: 1) Conjunctural causation: the effect of a single condition unfolds in combination with other conditions; 2) Equifinality: multiple configurations (or combinations) of conditions may lead to the same outcome; 3) Causal asymmetry: the causes leading to the presence of an outcome of interest may be quite different from those leading to the absence of the outcome....Configurational theorising instead studies the holistic effect stemming from a configuration (or combination) of causal conditions."[250]

As Pawson puts it, "the programme is not seen as a disembodied feature with its own causal powers. Rather, programmes are successful when...the right intervention type, with clear and pertinent objectives, comes into contact with an appropriate target group, and is administered and researched by an effective stakeholder alliance, working to common goals, in a conducive setting, and so on. This logic utilizes a 'configurational' approach to causality, in which outcomes are considered to follow from the alignment, within a case, of specific combinations of attributes."[251]

Some Problems With Realist Evaluations

Here we must keep in mind the fragile epistemological status of realist evaluations. While hundreds have been completed, some serious epistemological questions have not yet been resolved. A study of the Context-Mechanism-Outcome (CMO) formulation used by realist evaluators found that "three main types of challenges can be discerned: Difficulties distinguishing between

---

[250] Iannacci, F. & Kraus, S. (2023). "Configurational Theory: A review." In Papagiannidis, S. (ed). *TheoryHub Book*. Available at https://open.ncl.ac.uk.

[251] Pawson (2002). Op.cit. p. 173.

the different components of the CMO configuration, difficulties adequately capturing the complexity of mechanisms, and difficulties related to empirically validating CMOs."[252] Which is no small problem if realist evaluations are to help us understand a program, let alone be of practical use.

A recent review of the realist evaluation literature[253] revealed an unsettling lack of agreement on how mechanisms should be defined, with correspondingly different epistemic assumptions. And the problem already arises in Pawson and Tilley's seminal book, where they think about mechanisms in three ways—mechanisms as program components, mechanisms as participant reactions to program activities, and mechanisms as explanatory accounts[254]:

o *Mechanism as Program Components.* These are mechanisms that are not hidden, but directly observable as program elements that introduce "appropriate ideas and opportunities" to intended beneficiaries in the appropriate social and cultural context(s).

o *Mechanism as Participant Reactions to Program Components.* People do not change automatically the way a car changes direction when we turn the steering wheel. Rather, they change —i.e., make choices—in response to their subjective experiences (e.g., deciding whether and when and how far to turn the steering wheel), including how they perceive, think about, and understand program activities and the context(s) in which they are participating in them.

---

[252] Lemire, S., Kwako, A., Nielsen, S. B., Christie, C. A., Donaldson, S. I, & Leeuw, F. L. (2020). "What is this thing called a mechanism? Findings from a review of realist evaluations." In Schmitt, J. (ed.), *Causal Mechanisms in Program Evaluation. New Directions for Evaluation.* 167:73–86. p. 79.

[253] Ibid.

[254] Pawson R. & Tilley N. (1997). Op. cit.

o *Mechanism as Explanatory Accounts.* This conceptual-
ization looks at how mechanisms can be used as units
of analysis to explain program processes that produce
participant outcomes. Mechanisms are not to be con-
fused with program activities but rather are an account
of the often invisible, yet inductively identified processes which, in aggregate, are responsible for the production of outcomes within specific contexts.

Each of these versions of mechanisms asks questions that differ from those of the others and seeks to answer them accordingly.
Not surprisingly, this has had practical implications for the design
and implementation of realist evaluations. In a review of 195 realist
evaluations,[255] the authors found that 105 evaluations (53.8%) used
121 definitions of mechanism; one-third (33.9%) defined mechanisms as components or features of programs, and as such are seen as
constituent parts of the program; a further third (31.4%) saw mechanisms as examples of participants' reactions and ways of thinking
in response to program activities (or, possibly in response to other
program mechanisms); one fourth (24.0%) saw them as underlying
and thus unobservable (causal) processes; and finally, some (6.6%)
described mechanisms as theories that support inquiry into how
programs work.

The authors go on to examine which types of mechanisms
actually were used in their sample of 195 realist evaluations. They
found that a total of 126 (64.6%) were systematic in using the realist Context+Mechanism=Outcome (CMO) configuration; but
within these 126 evaluations, they found a notably large number of such CMO configurations—a total of 517 to be exact.
Even more confusing is the fact that "these CMO configurations

---

[255] Lemire, S,. Kwako, A., Nielsen, .S B, et al. (2020) Op. cit.

contained 827 context conditions, 904 mechanisms, and 678 outcomes."[256] How practical, how useful, is such a huge set of data points, is such a huge degree of disparate views somehow shoehorned into the "simple" CMO arrangement?

Nor is the problem resolved by Pawson and Tilley when they write that "a mechanism is thus not a variable but an account of the make-up, behavior, and interrelationships of those processes which are responsible for the regularity"[257] of outcome patterns. A statement that for me at least, resists parsing.

Furthermore, a very practical problem exists in empirically determining whether mechanisms are present or absent. This is due, at least in part, to the difficulty of developing testable CMO configurations—such as when the context is highly variable or when the mechanism is subconscious. The problem is made worse by the fact that often there are multiple plausible CMO configurations[258] as was illustrated above.

In summary, the difference between a mechanism and a program component or activity is a hard distinction even for realist evaluators to grasp and apply. As quoted in Asbury and Leeuw[259] Carol Weiss, an early advocate of theory-based evaluation, attempted to clarify the distinction using the example of a pregnancy reduction counseling program:

> [I]f counselling is associated with reduction in pregnancy, the cause of change might seem to be the counselling. But the mechanism is not the counselling; that is…the program process. The mechanism might be the knowledge

---

[256] Ibid. p. 77.

[257] Pawson, R. & Tilley, N.(2008). Op. cit. p. 68.

[258] Lemire, S., Kwako, A, Nielsen, S. B., et al. (2020). Op. cit.

[259] Asbury B. & Leeuw, F. L . (2010). Op. cit. p. 367.

that participants gain from the counselling. Or it might be that the existence of the counselling program helps to overcome cultural taboos against family planning; it might give women confidence and bolster their assertiveness in sexual relationships; it might trigger a shift in the power relations between men and women. These or any of several other cognitive, affective, social responses could be the mechanisms leading to desired outcomes.

While any or all of these explanations may be true, this elucidation seems at best fuzzy. It looks like anything at all could be a mechanism. This reflects an epistemic problem that realist evaluators still are discussing—namely, (a) what we can know about a program and the effects associated with it, (b) how one should proceed to learn about these things, and (c) how confident one should be about what one thinks one has learned. As mentioned above, some serious efforts to answer these questions are underway[260] but as yet are far from achieving this goal. As noted in a relevant article,

> The apparent confusion about the concept of mechanism demonstrates the need for continued conceptual and methodological discussion on the topic. Clearly the concept has seemed to many investigators to promise a fruitful, stimulating direction of inquiry…yet the range of definitions and modes of usage still present in the literature may undermine the benefits of the concept.[261]

Clearly, anyone who reads a realist evaluation report had better review the proffered definition of terms carefully—especially

---

[260] Greenhalgh T., Wong G., Jagosh J., et al. (2015). "Protocol—the RAMESES II study: developing guidance and reporting standards for realist evaluation." *BMJ Open* 5:e008567.

[261] Shaw, J., Gray, C. S., Baker, G. R., Denis, J.-L., Breton, M., Gutberg, J. Embuldeniya, G., Carswell, P., Dunham, A., McKillop, A., Kenealy, T., Sheridan, M., & Wodchis, W. (2018). "Mechanisms, contexts and points of contention: operationalizing realist informed research for complex health interventions. *BMC Medical Research Methodology*. Vol. 18:178.

regarding mechanisms. Otherwise, it will literally be impossible to know what the report is talking about.

A final but very important concern is that, unlike RCTs, realist evaluations do not have any built-in means for dealing with evaluation biases. This is because realist evaluations are themselves theories about how to evaluate theories and thus are not tied to manifest program data the way RCTs are. I believe that if pressed realist evaluators would argue that, given the wide range of data they consider, bias will be managed through "triangulation" or the use of their diverse data sets from varied sources to test their validity against each other. But this is at best a weak argument and, it seems to me, leaves wide open the front door for confirmation bias and other biases to march in and make themselves at home.

Some Examples of Realist Evaluations

Despite these unresolved issues, for certain kinds of explorations, especially when interventions and their contexts are complex, *realist evaluations can do the job if terms are defined clearly and operationally.* For example, a realist approach was used to evaluate an initiative to transform health services in London, England.[262] This involved evaluating a major change effort that "spanned four large health care organizations, covered three services (stroke, kidney, and sexual health), and sought to 'modernize' these services with a view to making health care more efficient, effective, and patient-centered."[263] The main focus was not on whether the transformation worked but rather to learn about the how the initiatives'

---

[262] Greenhalg, T., Humphrey, C., Hughes J., MacFarlane F., Butler, C. & Pawson, R. (2009). "How Do You Modernize a Health Service? A Realist Evaluation of Whole-Scale Transformation in London." *The Milbank Quarterly*, Vol. 87(2) pp. 391–416.

[263] Ibid. p. 391.

"fortunes were shaped, enabled, and constrained by the interaction of the context of the program and the chosen mechanisms of change."[264] The study identified key mechanisms of change and the contextual conditions that both supported and constrained them. The initiatives' accomplishments were listed as follows:

> Briefly…they include attention to cultural as well as structural changes; clarification of the resource implications of the new or altered services; the development of strategies for retaining skills and expertise within the local health economy; plans for the continued involvement of users; the maintenance of links with voluntary sector and partner organizations; and a sustained interorganizational structure for governance and formal communication.[265]

Similarly, a realist evaluation was conducted to assess the reform of adolescent health services in Ecuador.[266] It was

> …based on three health services located in different settings in Ecuador…and [designed] to explore four interconnected aspects: (i) the interventions carried out to improve adolescents' access to these services, (ii) the contexts local, institutional and national in which these interventions were implemented, (iii) the outcomes achieved in terms of accessibility/acceptability, good quality/relevance and gender equality, and (iv) the mechanisms that triggered the transformation of three 'ordinary' health services into what are currently considered as national models of AFSs [adolescent-friendly services].[267]

---

[264] Ibid. p. 395.

[265] Ibid. p. 410.

[266] Goicolea, I., Coe, A.-B., Hurtig, A. K. & Sebastian, M. S. (2012). "Mechanisms for Achieving Adolescent-Friendly Services in Ecuador: a realist evaluation approach." Glob Health Action. Vol. 5:18748.

[267] Ibid. reference page 3.

Working inductively from collected interviews and focus groups (as well as some quantifiable data on youth participation that, due to low numbers, could not be analyzed in a statistically significant manner) the researchers were able to identify which centers were succeeding in improving youth participation and what mechanisms they were employing to do so. They subsequently used these data to develop guidelines for improving youth services across the country.

> The New Guidelines promoted comprehensive care for adolescents' health, based on: (i) differentiated services delivered with a comprehensive, intercultural, participatory and rights-based approach; and (ii) friendly care encompassing respect, confidentiality and providers with positive attitudes, skills and competencies. The Guidelines stressed the importance of considering gender issues during the planning and implementation of services, and stressed that health services could and should contribute to gender equality. [268]

---

[268] Ibid. reference page 5.

Chapter XII

RESEARCH SYNTHESES
OF AGGREGATED PROGRAM EFFECTS

As suggested previously, realist evaluations in themselves don't solve the problem of rendering their causal findings plausible in the United States, although they seem to have done so in the rest of the world. Instead of comparing programs with counterfactuals and calculating the statistical probability that differences in outcomes are due to the program, their standard practice is to repeat evaluations in continuous cycles and look for accumulating patterns of evidence about the likelihood that observed outcomes are being produced contingently by mechanisms in specific contexts. *The persistent question in every realist evaluation is when enough such iterative evidence has been accumulated that reasonable causal assumptions can be reached.* Of course, there is no right answer, no dispositive number. All one can say is, the more the better—until we run out of resources or patience. But that is not the kind of dispositive answer many evaluation stakeholders might like if it were presented to them.

Of course, this situation also arises with RCTs. As we have seen in Chapter VIII, RCTs also don't really solve the problem of how plausible their findings are. After all, a p-value of 0.05 is an arbitrary cutoff; it is an interpretive decision—nothing more nor less. Here too the ideal solution would be to replicate an RCT evaluation multiple times to see if the findings hold. But this is rarely done for social program evaluations, nor is it likely to be an adopted practice in the foreseeable future.

So it turns out that the same questions arise for both realist and RCT evaluations: "Can we somehow compensate for the fact that single studies can at best provide highly tentative answers?" and "If so, what can be done?" Many evaluators have concluded that the obvious choice is not to settle on the findings of any single program evaluation—whether realist or RCT—but to look across all relevant evaluations and analyze them synthetically. Such studies, when analyzing RCT-based impact data, are referred to as *meta-analyses*; where the findings of realist evaluations are used these studies are called *synthetic reviews*.

Returning to the Problem of Plausible Program Causality

How can evaluators produce such cross-cutting syntheses? The accepted way is to produce analytical syntheses of published evaluations that are aggregated based on program similarities. Cross-program analyses then are used to identify strong enough outcome patterns that they can be considered generalizable; that is, sufficiently important to inform decisions—for example, about what kinds of programs to support or replicate.

As mentioned above, The Institute of Education Sciences, the What Works Clearinghouse, the Cochran Library, and its online open access journal Cochrane Evidence Synthesis and Methods, and the Campbell Collaboration all give priority to *syntheses over the findings of individual evaluations.* And indeed the use of systematic reviews has ballooned.

> In the period January 1, 1986 to December 4, 2015, PubMed tags 266,782 items as "systematic reviews" and 58,611 as "meta-analyses." Annual publications between 1991 and 2014 increased 2,728% for systematic reviews and 2,635% for meta-analyses versus only 153% for all PubMed-indexed items. Currently, probably more systematic reviews of trials than new randomized trials are published annually.[269]

Let's look at the two kinds of syntheses in turn, starting with meta-analyses.

Quantitative Meta-Analyses

Quantitative meta-analyses of social program evaluations evolved from evidence-based medicine where the purpose is to look for effective treatments of diseases and other disorders. This approach requires that the analyst carefully classify the programs under review by program family or types within a family by *the kinds of outcomes they are intended to produce.* In the social domain, this requires that analysts identify a specific program family they want to study. So they would look at "work-readiness programs" that are intended to improve employability; "school attendance programs" intended to drive down absenteeism; "literacy programs" intended to improve reading scores; "recidivism reduction programs" intended to lower repetitive incarceration rates; and so on. The analyst produces a clear map of the outcomes produced by each member of the program family (or types within a family) and then combines them across

---

[269] Ioannidis, J. P. A. (2016). "The Mass Production of Redundant, Misleading, and Conflicted Systematic Reviews and Meta-analyses." *The Milbank Quarterly.* September.

programs to show the aggregated net effect of the programs within a given family that individually are working to address the same (or very similar) outcomes.

The unit of analysis is the relevant family of programs.[270] A database is compiled of published program evaluations within each such grouping, and then ascertaining each program's reported net effect. From these facts, the mean effect aggregated for each program family is calculated. The mean effect, then, becomes the answer to whether a given program family "works"—and is seen as stronger evidence than the impacts that are found in a single program evaluation. The intent is that policymakers and funders will use such research to support or replicate those kinds of programs that appear strongest, and conversely steer resources away from programs that seem weak. [271] And the stakes are high:

> Like all of the best ideas, the big idea here is a simple one— that research should attempt to pass on collective wisdom about the successes and failures of previous initiatives in particular policy domains. The prize is also a big one in that such an endeavour could provide the antidote to policy-making's frequent lapses into crowd pleasing, political pandering, window dressing and good acting.[272]

There are, however, some notable limitations to meta-analyses.

The first is the reliance on the concept of program types or families. By what outcome criteria will programs be grouped together? By what criteria separated? Even within such categories, how much agreement is there about these criteria, about the definition of outcomes used to categorize programs? And as Aristotle taught

---

[270] Sometimes, however, the analysis will be confined to a type of program within a larger family.

[271] Pawson, R. (2002). Op. cit. p. 341.

[272] Pawson, R. (2002). Ibid. p. 160.

us, categorization inevitably involves exclusion (of outliers), and exclusion inherently leads to simplification. In a positivist epistemic framework, such simplification is accepted as a reasonable price to pay. But as we will see shortly, this is less so in a realist framework where things we cannot observe directly and therefore must infer inductively[273] nevertheless have a place—and with which, therefore, one must reckon.

But there is even a more fundamental source of simplification in meta-analyses: as was discussed in Chapters VI and VIII, the very nature of the data that individual RCTs produce inherently are themselves highly simplified; and then the simplifications of the meta-analyses are built on top of them. Simplifications on top of simplifications. Indeed, in practice, meta-analyses can have us scratching our heads about what each category of data actually means in operational terms. So let's look at these matters in a bit more detail.[274]

Meta-Analyses Tend to Merge Program Elements that Drive Change

Within a family of programs, there is likely to be a great deal of overlap in the utilization of program components, the elements of program design that are depended on to produce desired results for program participants. So, for example, many work readiness programs will include as an element "teaching soft skills." These are adaptive skills that are seen as essential for people to master in order to function successfully in any work setting. They include such

---

[273] Just the way physicists working in cosmology have inferred the presence of dark mass and dark energy, presumed entities that inherently cannot be observed directly.

[274] The following observations are grounded in a recent effort where I was part of a team partnering with a major evaluation shop to produce a meta-analysis of programs working with disconnected young people.

things as showing up on time, dressing appropriately, taking responsibility for completing work as assigned, being a valued teammate, and so on. But which of these does each program actually teach or emphasize? Which does it ignore? And how does it go about teaching them: Didactically? Experientially? Both? In what settings? Is cognitive behavioral therapy used? Motivational Interviewing?

It is safe to say that no two programs will be fully alike; and it's also safe to say that we really don't have much of a handle on what the differences among them mean, how they affect the readiness or ability of program participants to learn and apply these skills. So, what can we really say we "know" about programs that have the "same" elements? The analysis will by its very nature not explore such differences in depth because it is seeking commonalities and in doing so will simplify greatly and distort what they treat as "real" accordingly. "In short, the categories of metaanalysis [sic] have the potential to hide, within and between themselves, very many significant capacities for generating personal and social change and we thus need to be extremely careful, therefore, about making any causal imputations to any particular 'category'."[275]

Meta-Analyses Tend to Oversimplify Program Outcomes

Just because a program names the outcomes it is seeking to engender among participants does not necessarily mean that other programs using the same names for their outcomes mean the same things by them. How, to continue our case, will a given work readiness program identify "full employment" as the intended benefit to participants? Forty hours of work per week? Thirty? With benefits?

---

[275] Pawson, R. (2002). Op. cit. p. 165.

Without? If programs within a type are using different definitions for their outcomes, what then does it mean to look at "average" or "net" effects within a program family? Here again, the need to aggregate what may be very different things as they play out in the lives of individuals requires high-level simplification—and produces what in all probability will be a spurious precision in the presentation of findings. "This is the second problem with numerical metaanalysis [sic], concealed in that rather tight-fisted term—the 'mean effect'. The crucial point to recall as we cast our eyes down the outputs of metaanalysis…is that the figures contained therein are means of means of means of means! It is useful to travel up the chain of aggregation to examine how exactly the effect calculations are performed for each sub-category of a programme."[276]

Meta-Analyses Tend to Ignore Program Contexts

As discussed above, RCTs are explicitly designed to use a counterfactual and thereby look past the effects of contexts on program delivery—and perhaps even more importantly, on program participants. Contexts may well have differing effects on individual participants, such as to what degree they identify with or trust the staff who are working with them or how they feel about some of the activities in which they are expected to participate. Even the design of a given venue may affect program participants in dissimilar ways. "No individual-level intervention works for everyone. No institution-level intervention works everywhere. The net effect of any particular programme is thus made up of the balance of successes and failures of individual subjects and locations. Thus any 'programme outcome'—single, pooled or mean—depends not merely upon 'the programme' but also on its subjects and its circumstances. *These contextual*

---

[276] Ibid.

variations are yet another feature that is squeezed out of the picture in the aggregation process of metaanalysis"[277] (emphasis in original).

Meta-Analyses are Confined to Examining What Has Been Published

And here we have a serious problem for meta-analyses: the fact that, for obvious reasons, they only scan published evaluation studies. But that's a big problem because, as we have been warned by a leading research methodologist, *"most published research findings are false"*[278] (emphasis added).

Here it is worth remembering that perhaps the most powerful evaluation bias of all is publication bias: the deliberate suppression of negative evaluation findings by journal editors (because negative findings are hardly captivating news); by evaluators themselves (because they know such findings are unlikely to get published); and by program funders (because they don't want to waste money or perhaps just because they don't want to look foolish), to name only the most obvious. So "hidden diversity in outcome measures follows from the possibility that certain indicators (cynics may guess which!) may have been used but have gone unreported in the original studies, given limitations on journal space and pressures to report successful outcomes."[279]

For some evaluators, the solution to these problems lies in conducting what they call "second-level meta-analyses." These produce statistical meta-regressions that are causal models which identify correlations between program participant characteristics and outcomes. "This approach goes beyond the idea of finding mean effects

---

[277] Ibid. p. 166.

[278] Ioannidis, J. P. A. (2005). Op. cit.

[279] Pawson, N. (2002). Op. cit. p. 165.

for a particular class of treatment. It assumes, correctly, that the average is made up of a range of different effects, coloured by such factors as: 1) the characteristics of the clients; 2) the length or intensity of the treatment; and even 3) the type of design in the original study. Studies attempting to identify such 'mediators' and 'moderators'…do make an undoubted leap forward…"[280]

Realist Syntheses

In general, realist syntheses or reviews have the same goals as meta-analyses. But they look at evaluations across a given family or type of program mechanism, not at a whole program, to find out "what works." To whit:

> …it is not programmes that work but the resources they offer to enable their subjects to make them work. This process of how subjects interpret the intervention stratagem is known as the programme 'mechanism' and it is the pivot around which realist evaluation revolves. So…let us consider the causal powers of programmes offering 'transitional payments' to prisoners on release with the aim of preventing the need for a quick return to crime. In such cases, it is not the programme that causes 'rehabilitation'. It merely provides payments, which the subjects choose to use in different ways, one of which might be to steer away from crime….Since it is 'programme mechanisms' that trigger change rather than 'programmes' as such, then it is much more sensible to base any systematic review on 'families of mechanisms' rather than on 'families of programmes'. This gives realist synthesis a completely different locus of comparison from the other methods of systematic review. The starting point is to refrain from tackling original evaluations that belong to particular 'families of interventions'….Rather, realist synthesis takes on

---

[280] Ibid. p. 169.

'families of mechanisms' (e.g. the same programme theory, say 'incentivization', implemented across the domains of health, education, crime, welfare, employment and so on). The importance of such a strategy is that it solves one of the key dilemmas of systematic review, namely that of achieving a proper comparison of 'like with like'.[281]

Kinds of Information that are Relevant to Realist Syntheses

Realist syntheses examine the data used for the original realist evaluations: records of one-on-one interviews of relevant stakeholders; focus groups of stakeholders; case studies of series of interventions; and direct observations of specific interventions with selected individuals. All these data, of course, will be coded and analyzed using qualitative data management software.

Just as individual realist evaluations focus on processes and relationships in order to explore whether something happens and, of equal importance, why and how it is happening "on the ground," so realist syntheses try to establish the nature of the mechanisms that seem to drive outcomes in a given family of programs that feature them. They will specify what, for a given analysis, is considered to be context; what interventions with what mechanisms will be considered; and which outcomes will be tracked. In other words, *the data will be about the relationships among things*, not about the things in themselves (i.e., a program and its component parts). Such data will not be quantified easily, especially since to a large extent they will be qualitative; and where they are quantified, the act of categorizing and quantifying them inevitably will involve simplifying them, just as with quantitative meta-analyses.

---

[281] Pawson, R. (2002). Op. cit. p. 343.

And just as with meta-analyses, realist syntheses rely on published studies as their data sources; so here too we must be deeply concerned about publication bias and even more, perhaps, about confirmation bias because of the strongly subjective nature of realist evaluations.

Furthermore, it is fair to say that a great deal of patience and perseverance is needed to maintain analytical standards while examining dozens or even hundreds of intervention mechanisms. Here too we find a fertile ground for research bias. Which brings us to the analyses themselves.

Still Incomplete: How to do Realist Syntheses

Early narrative syntheses tried to create an abstract for each evaluation being considered and mapped these in a matrix in order to find recurring themes or patterns inductively. Of course, where the data were qualitative, this meant populating the matrix cells with text—including anything from key quotations taken from the original studies to the analyst's responses to the material. Analyzing such heterogeneous data sets can be daunting, to say the least. This has led to the still ongoing development of more systematized methods of analysis where studies are considered in relation to a common, crosscutting analytical framework.[282] A more stark way of saying this is that there are currently no generally accepted nor widely used quality standards for realist syntheses—which is hardly surprising since this also is true for the analytical methods used in the underlying individual realist evaluations.

---

[282] Greenhalgh T., Wong G., Jagosh J., Greenhalg, J., Manzano, A., Westhorp G., & Pawson, R. (2015). Op. cit.

Summary: Synthetic Research

Both statistical meta-analyses and realist reviews offer syntheses of what evaluations have uncovered about programs and their effectiveness across but within limited domains, and as such tell us more than any individual evaluation can provide. But while this can be useful, neither can "prove" anything. Within their respective epistemic frameworks, these syntheses really tell us stories that are made plausible to us because of the cultural worlds we inhabit, and how well the kinds of findings they proffer conform to the cause-and-effect assumptions that our culture's metaphysical world takes for granted. They seem so utterly "scientific."

And once again we have to remind ourselves of the prevalence and grave distortions of publication bias which, more than we might fully appreciate, promotes confirmation bias and at times actual research fraud. Again, Ioannidis discussing synthetic reviews:

> Publication of systematic reviews and meta-analyses has increased rapidly. These meta-analyses are often produced either by industry employees or by authors with industry ties and results are aligned with sponsor interests....Furthermore, many contracting companies working on evidence synthesis receive industry contracts to produce meta-analyses, many of which probably remain unpublished. Many other meta-analyses have serious flaws. Of the remaining, most have weak or insufficient evidence to inform decision making. *Few systematic reviews and meta-analyses are both non-misleading and useful*[283] (emphasis added).

In point of fact, there is considerable concern among researchers that published studies that subsequently had to be retracted in retrospect due to the post-publication discovery of serious problems

---

[283] Ioannidis, J. P. A. (2016). Op. cit.

with their data, often are left as data points in systematic reviews even after these problems have been established. It is also likely that removing such studies could change the conclusions the reviews reach—and ultimately stimulate rethinking of decisions that have been based on them.[284] Which might well be upsetting to key stakeholders especially, one might hazard, with regard to programs receiving public support.

With all these considerations in mind, and with some sadness, I find it impossible to disagree with Ioannidis who has suggested that quite possibly "the large majority of produced systematic reviews and meta-analyses are unnecessary, misleading, and/or conflicted."[285]

---

[284] Noorden, R. v. (2023). "How Many Clinical Trials Can't be Trusted?" *Nature*. Vol. 619. 20 July. pp. 454-458.

[285] Ibid.

Chapter XIII

COMPARISON OF RCTs
AND REALIST EVALUATIONS

In comparing RCTs and realist evaluations, it is important to remember what kinds of causal explanations each supports. RCTs mostly utilize (a) counterfactual and (b) successionist understandings of causation. In contrast, realist evaluations are grounded in (a) generative and (b) configurational thinking. However, both approaches rely on research methods designed to produce what, in the epistemic frameworks within which they operate, is "true" information about programs and their impacts.

The table on the following pages looks across both approaches and captures the relevant qualities of each—the intent being to inform decision-making when an evaluation method is being selected.

Table 1. Comparison of RCTs and Realist Evaluations

Key Characteristics	RCT Evaluations	Realist Evaluations
Ontological description of a program – the evaluation's operational view of it, including the cause-and-effect assumptions that drive the evaluation's methods	*Programs are relatively static, fully observable entities with borders that are managed intentionally.* They consist of regularly occurring activities that may be combined to form program elements; the program as a whole is the set of all its prescribed elements. *There is a linear sequential cause-and-effect assumption*: Program outputs produce program effects (outcomes) for program participants. Contextual contributions to the production of outcomes are disposed of analytically through the use of a counterfactual.	*Programs are theories manifested social systems (with the inherent dynamism and permeability of boundaries that all human systems exhibit).* They feature dynamic configurations of contexts, mechanisms, and outcomes. Cause and effect is assumed to vary across and be dependent on context. It is understood to operate generatively in terms of Context-Mechanisms-Outcomes configurations. *Thus causality is never straightforward, but rather relational and contingent.*
Epistemic framework for the evaluation	Positivism	Realism
Overall approach	Instrumentalist	Essentialist
Situations for which the method is best suited	Relatively simple program designs typically represented in an *inputs—outputs—outcomes* sequence, and in relatively simple contexts.	From simple to very complex program designs, all of which are represented in *context—mechanism—outcomes* configurations, and often employed in complex contexts.
Major kinds of data that are utilized	In practice, generally quantitative plus (sometimes) complementary qualitative data.	In practice, generally qualitative plus (in some cases) complementary quantitative data.

Key Characteristics	RCT Evaluations	Realist Evaluations
Analytical methodology	1. Experimental 2. Deductive	1. Case study 2. Inductive
Major methods used to investigate causality	1. Counterfactual 2. Successionist	1. Generative 2. Configurational
Cause and effect assumptions they make	Linear. The program and its components produce changes in participants (or fail to do so); the program either works or it doesn't, with context being neutralized using the concept of "treatment as usual".	Relational. The context has an impact on the mechanisms that inspire and influence program participants to achieve intended changes (or fail to do so); the mechanisms either are effective or not in a contextually contingent manner (they are activated or inhibited by contextual conditions) with individuals whose differences influence receptivity to program mechanisms must thus be taken into account.
Approach to studying probability	Frequentist (though rarely discussed using this name)	Bayesian (though not expressly acknowledged)
Analytical method used to increase confidence in the assessment of a programs' effectiveness	Statistical meta-analyses	Realist syntheses
Units of analysis	(1) Program as a whole, (2) Program elements, and (3) Program net effect outcomes	Hypotheses generated by program theories that are studied by repetitively looking for patterns with regard to (1) Context, (2) Mechanisms, and (3) Participant outcomes

Key Characteristics	RCT Evaluations	Realist Evaluations
Questions an evaluation answers	(1) What were the demographic and risk indicators of program participants? (2) What were the program elements and dosages delivered to participants? (3) What were the participants' outcomes? (4) What was the effect size? (5) What is the probability that these outcomes were produced by the program? Bottom line: Did the program Work? Answered quantitatively and deductively.	(1) What was/were the context(s) in which the intervention was evaluated? (2) What were the demographic and risk indicators of program participants at each iteration? (3) What was the intervention (what were the program elements and dosages delivered to participants)? (4) What were the mechanisms influencing program participants to achieve intended outcomes? (5) What were the participants' outcomes? Bottom line: For whom did the program work, why, and in what contexts? Answered qualitatively and inductively.
Approach to context as an explanatory factor	Context is managed down as an explanatory factor using the concept of Treatment as Usual (TAU) that would be available to all individuals studied, with the differences in outcomes for program participants *versus* counterfactual control group participants providing the basis for estimating the probability and size of program effects.	Context is seen as working catalytically to stimulate and support the effectiveness of intervention mechanisms to help program recipients achieve outcomes as intended, and/or as inhibitors of these processes.

The picture, it seems fair to say, is muddled for both RCTs and realist evaluations—but for different reasons. RCTs are used to explore "what works" among social programs. Their findings—highly quantitative in nature—can provide a first step in learning about social programs and their effects. However, they often offer a spurious precision about what we know and can learn. In doing so, they may lead to dispositive decisions about which programs to support or even to replicate, as well as which to abandon; and often such decisions are made confidently when instead they should be made with great caution.

Realist evaluations, in demonstrating repeatedly how tentative what we know and can learn must always be—how ephemeral reality (as we understand it) is—consequently can be confusing and will not support operational decisions dispositively. But they will help us understand—partially and provisionally—how programs seem to be working (or not), for whom, using which mechanisms, and in what contexts; and thereby suggest how they might be improved.

The contrast between the two evaluation approaches discussed here can be summarized in a nutshell:

RCTs and their meta-analyses, in relying predominantly on quantitative data, emphasize form over content.

Realist evaluations and their syntheses, in relying to a large extent on qualitative data, emphasize content over form.

Chapter XIV

THE PROMISE OF MIXED METHODS

Today most evaluators, including those who see the world through positivist lenses, understand the utility of using what are called "mixed methods" in program evaluations. Their oft-repeated adage is *"No numbers without stories, no stories without numbers."* Why? Because numbers without stories that explain them are not especially meaningful, while stories without numbers contextualizing them are not necessarily relevant. There is notable literature on this subject[286], including the useful textbook by Creswell and Clark, *Designing and Conducting Mixed Methods Research.*[287]

Realist Trials—Combining RCTs and Realist Evaluations

The obvious question thus arises: Can RCTs and realist evaluations be combined meaningfully? This turns out to be a simple question to ask—but a complex one to answer. In doing so I am

---

[286] Greene, J. C. (2015). "The emergence of mixing methods in the field of evaluation." *Qualitative Health Research*,. Vol. 25(6), pp. 746–750.

[287] Creswell, J. W. & Clark, V. L. P. (2017). *Designing and Conducting Mixed Methods Research*. Sage.

indebted to the recent article by Nielsen, Jaspers, and Lemire[288] who use the term *realist trial* to denote the intentional combining of realist evaluations and experimental research methods (RCTs). "Over the past 10 years," they observe, "realist trials have been proposed as an evaluation approach that combines the strengths of RCTs in providing evidence on what works with the explanatory strength of REs [realist evaluations] to describe *how, under what circumstances, and for whom they work*"[289] (emphasis in original).

However, the possibility of joining RCTs and realist evaluations together is, in itself, a contentious proposition. In fact, some realist thinkers have characterized the very idea as oxymoronic. They see the problem as both epistemic and ontological: as they see it, positivist RCTs using successionist and counterfactual concepts of causality are not in any obvious way compatible with realist evaluations that take configurational and generative approaches to understanding causal dynamics.[290]

Yet despite these conceptual challenges, there are now numerous instances of evaluators attempting to conduct mixed-method realist trials to evaluate programs.[291] This led to the third-party examination of such attempts by Nielsen, Jaspers, and Lemire who were cited above.[292] In all, they reviewed 16 realist trials. Of these,

---

[288] Nielsen, S. B., Jaspers, S. O. & Lemire, S. (2023). "The curious case of the realist trial: Methodological oxymoron or unicorn?" *Evaluation*. Sage. DOI: 10.1177/13563890231200291. Access at: https://doi.org/10.1177/13563890231200291.

[289] Ibid. p. 2.

[290] Ibid.

[291] Nielsen S. B., Lemire, S. & Tangsig, S. (2022). "Unpacking context in realist evaluations: Findings from a comprehensive review." *Evaluation* 28(1): 91–112.

[292] Nielsen, S. B., Jaspers, S. O. & Lemire, S. (2023). Op. cit.

only six had realist evaluation components that fully met the RAMESES Common Standards for realist evaluations.[293] And of those six, only three had RCT components that were implemented at a high level of quality. So out of the 16 studies reviewed, only three showed good quality in both their RCT and realist evaluation components.[294] At this time, it seems, the desirability of conjoined realist trials is more conceptually compelling than achieved.

But let's look at a couple of examples where such realist trials have been successful. One studied patients' decisions to taper down or withdraw completely from medications in collaboration with their physicians to reduce adverse side effects and improve outcomes—a process known as "deprescribing."[295] The study looked at deprescribing from the patient's point of view. A realist evaluation was conducted alongside a large RCT that examined the effectiveness of a direct-to-consumer, written educational brochure called EMPOWER which was mailed to patients who, it was hoped, would subsequently discontinue their sedative-hypnotic medication.[296] As the study's researchers put it, the use of "a mixed methods approach enabled us to explore the breadth, depth and complexity of the patient's experience of deprescribing." To which they added, "Use of the realist evaluation allowed us to investigate how the mechanisms underlying deprescribing interventions interact with specific contexts to yield positive or negative outcomes."[297]

---

[293] Greenhalgh T., Pawson R., Wong G., et al. (2016). Op. cit.

[294] Ibid. Table 4, p. 9.

[295] Martin P, Tannenbaum C. (2017). "A realist evaluation of patients' decisions to deprescribe in the EMPOWER trial." *BMJ Open.*

[296] Ibid. p. 2.

[297] Ibid. p. 1.

The evaluation identified the following mechanisms that, singly or in combination for a given patient, triggered his or her motivation to deprescribe:

1. Increasing knowledge and concern about benzodiazepines;

2. Augmenting patients' capacity and self-efficacy to taper benzodiazepines; and

3. Creating opportunities for the patient to discuss and receive support from a healthcare provider to engage in the deprescribing process.[298]

Another example of an RCT used along with realist evaluation methods involves an evaluation of "The Mental Health Link," a complex intervention for shared care in mental health that was designed to improve services provided by family doctors working in primary health care teams, and community mental health workers in community mental health teams.[299]

The multi-faceted Mental Health Link intervention was subjected to a cluster RCT, with randomisation by practice. The proposed components of shared care included: primary care-based systems for registers, recall, and review; education and audit; and the development of a liaison relationship with specialists...Delivery of organisational change was dependent on three fixed components: training of facilitators, a toolkit and small financial incentives. The toolkit included: a guide through a series of meetings attended by representatives of both teams and service users; instructions for creating registers, carrying out audits and assessing educational needs; and a flexible template for

---

[298] Ibid.

[299] Byng, R., Norman, I., Redfern, S. & Jones, R. (2008). "Exposing the key functions of a complex intervention for shared care in mental health: A case study of a process evaluation." *BMC Health Services Research*. Vol. 8. p. 274.

a written shared care agreement between providers, detailing allocation of responsibilities and protocols for formal communication. In contrast, the actual work of the facilitator was designed to be explicitly flexible, responding to the context of primary care, specialist teams and health needs, but encouraging both teams to develop shared care in line with the proposed model. Similarly the role of the linked specialist worker for each practice would depend on local context.[300]

The study looked at the relationships between the fixed and flexible components of the intervention, and their collective relationship with the external context. It was hypothesized that contextual elements can modify the effects achievable by the reformed healthcare services and consequently the anticipated health outcomes. The following description of the study provides a detailed example of how a realist evaluation proceeds through a series of hypothesis tests:

> Provisional causal hypotheses, ready to be tested using the analytic induction process, were derived both from themes emerging during the initial coding process, and by examining the matrix for obvious patterns. Each provisional hypothesis was further developed by systematically assessing it against first the positive and then the negative cases in the matrix, and adapting it by incorporating further contextual factors and mechanisms to describe how each overall outcome of shared care developed. Alternatively they were rejected if the data did not support the provisional hypothesis. These more refined theories about how and why services had developed, incorporating the interaction between context and mechanisms, were then rechecked against the original transcripts and further refined if necessary. Lastly, the refined hypotheses were examined together to look for overarching themes

---

[300] Ibid. p. 3.

explaining the key functions of the intervention, both those relating to shared care for mental health, and those relating to successfully achieving change.[301]

I will give the final word on mixed method, realist trials to Nielsen, Jasper, and Lemire:

> Realist trials are breaking new, contentious ground. Along with new ideas and new approaches, questions will inevitably arise. While the current review does not resolve underlying philosophical differences, the review did reveal relatively few cases that managed to design both a high-quality RCT and RE. If realist trials are to evolve from its infancy, there is a clear need to catalog designs that integrate RE and RCT, and along with it, analytical approaches that make full use of quantitative and qualitative data....In this review, we found some cases that successfully merged the two designs, or embedded REs within RCTs without compromising design quality....Continuing to insist that merging is not possible would therefore entail a responsibility to bring forward exemplary cases and rigorous methods that bring the evolution of RE alone forward.[302]

Some Final Thoughts on "Mixed Methods"

I have focused my discussion of evaluations using "mixed" quantitative and qualitative research methods on so-called realist trials where realist evaluations are combined with RCTs. In doing so I have chosen not to discuss "mixed methods" in program evaluation more generically because the decision to complement RCTs with some qualitative research is a simple one to reach and likely will be applauded by most stakeholders. However, the facile assumption

---

[301] Ibid. p. 4.

[302] Nielsen, S. B., Jaspers, S. O. & Lemire, S. (2023). Op. cit. pp. 15-16.

that both research methods have been undertaken at high levels of quality may, in any given instance, be mistaken, as the review of realist trials revealed.[303] So the use of "mixed methods" may provide a false sense of security to stakeholders who will want to make use of them for their diverse purposes.

Furthermore, while such studies generally do discuss the RCT and qualitative methods utilized in the evaluation, rarely is any attention paid to the fact that not only are two very different kinds of research methods being used, but two profoundly different epistemologies as well. Whereas it is not much of a challenge to understand the work of the two methods undertaken side by side, it's a much different story to consider what such combined methods can and can't reveal, can and can't teach us due to their respective epistemic limitations. The studies that I have read have, in seems to me, generally been presented in ways that take for granted their having covered all the bases. Epistemologically speaking, a risky proposition.

---

[303] Nielsen, S. B., Jaspers, S. O. & Lemire, S. (2023). Ibid.

Chapter XV

EMBRACING UTILIZATION FOCUSED EVALUATION

Although I have suggested it in various ways, it needs to be said explicitly: this work is an argument in favor of the principles of *utilization-focused evaluation*. As Michael Quinn Patton puts it, this approach "is evaluation done for and with specific intended primary users for specific, intended uses. [It] begins with the premise that evaluations should be judged by their utility and actual use; therefore, evaluators should…design any evaluation with careful consideration for how everything that is done, from beginning to end, will affect use."[304] Or, as I have argued elsewhere, evaluation should be considered a part of, and always be in service to, the management of social programs' performance: their quality, effectiveness, and reliability.[305] Accordingly, utilization-focused evaluation deals with epistemology pragmatically: epistemic assumptions and beliefs are clarified whenever necessary in relation to the nature of the questions to be answered by an evaluation of a particular program.

---

[304] Patton, M. Q. (2008). Op. cit. p. 37.

[305] Hunter, D. E. K. & Nielsen, S. B. (2013). "Performance Management and Evaluation: Exploring Complementarities." In Nielsen, S. B. & Hunter, D. E. K. (Eds.) (2013). Op.cit. pp. 7-17.

Evaluations As High Stakes Undertakings

So far this book has looked at some of the strategies that evaluators employ and examined their epistemic foundations. I hope that this will promote an understanding of, and elevate for consideration, some of the consequences of these assumptions and beliefs, especially as they affect how programs are designed, implemented, analyzed, understood, managed, and evaluated.

In general, it is undeniable that program evaluations tend to be rather expensive—although new, much less costly methods using artificial intelligence (AI) that rely on tapping enormous public data sets are emerging. But even if we put expense aside, in the social sector evaluations are undertaken with high stakes in mind —such as "proving" that a given program "works" and therefore should attract revenues to support it, in justifying the expansion of a given program to new sites, and in creating an evidentiary basis for disseminating knowledge about "what works" to help various populations improve their lives and prospects. So clearly programs undergoing evaluation also are facing a big risk because there is always the possibility that an evaluation may also "prove" that the program "doesn't work."

The fact that, logically speaking, an evaluation inherently cannot prove anything, is almost beside the point when it comes to what actually goes on in the social sector. For example, in February 2003 the evaluation firm Mathematica released its first-year report on the 3-year RCT it was hired to undertake of the federally funded 21st Century Community Learning Centers, a program dedicated to providing after-school services to both inner city and rural schoolchildren. In this report, *Mathematica stated explicitly that these early findings should be treated as highly provisional and that no decisions about the program should be based on them.* However, politics trumped reason. Because the report showed no evidence of improved academic outcomes for participants, the George W. Bush administration quickly announced plans to cut its federal funding by $400 million—a full 40% of the $1 billion that had been appropriated to fund it.

In the resulting uproar, several troubling things happened:

o   The Mathematica study was immediately subjected to intense criticism by leading youth development advocates.

o   These advocates, in lobbying to have the funding restored, adopted a dismissive stance toward the use of any evaluation data for setting funding priorities.

o   Members of the evaluation profession also were drawn into the fray. Some very publicly (and using uncharacteristically dogmatic and harsh language) attacked the methods and validity of the Mathematica study. But others rose vigorously in Mathematica's defense.

o   The funding ultimately was restored as a result of intensive lobbying—in which *the legitimate uses of evaluation data to inform social policy development and funding decisions were left undiscussed*—and hence evaluation once again was relegated to the margins of social utility in the domain of social programs.[306]

It is also worth noticing an extremely important context that makes evaluation a high-stakes undertaking: the uses that our

---

[306] I was asked to review this incident at the time. I found that the Mathematica study was strong, and I criticized the Bush administration for acting dispositively on evidence that was clearly provisional and incomplete. So the government's quick reversal of its initial decision to cut the program's budget by $400M was not based on any rational consideration of the case; rather it was based on political counter-pressure that the original decision generated.

courts make of research findings. So much do they do so that the Federal Judicial Center and the National Research Council jointly produce the *Reference Manual on Scientific Evidence*.[307] It provides conceptual tools for judges to manage complex cases where the potential exists for various "expert witnesses" to disagree with each other regarding the scientific standing of the "evidence-based" positions being argued. Recognizing that science is not a coherent, monolithic repository of knowledge that is applicable across all scientific domains, the Manual provides a unique set of standards for each scientific discipline it reviews (including epidemiology, toxicology, medicine, mental health, neuroscience, and engineering).[308]

But one standard does cut across all these disciplines. Only positivist, quantified research data are recognized. This stance had its origins in the seminal case of Daubert et al. v. Merrell Dow Pharmaceuticals which was heard by the U.S. Supreme Court in 1993.[309] The plaintiffs argued that the medication Benedictin was not safe for the public to use, and brought forward some highly respected experts who gave their personal opinion in support of the plaintiffs. Merrell Dow Pharmaceuticals, the drug's manufacturer, brought into evidence a large number of published research studies that showed no evidence that Benedictin was unsafe. The court decided to exclude from consideration the plaintiff's experts whose testimony was based solely on their opinions. Specifically, it held that "scientific evidence is admissible only if the principle on which

---

[307] The Federal Judicial Center & the National Research Council. (2011). *Reference Manual on Scientific Evidence*. 3rd Edition. The National Academies Press.

[308] I am grateful to Jonathan Borak, an epidemiologist who often testifies in such matters, for bringing the Daubert case and the Judicial Center's *Reference Manual* to my attention.

[309] Daubert v. Merril (1993). 509 U.S. 579.

it is based is 'sufficiently established to have general acceptance in the field to which it belongs.'"[310]

Things to Consider When Choosing a Program Evaluation Method

First off, we must accept that RCTs are the most well-formalized, elegant, and efficient method we have for assessing quantitatively the *probability* that a program as designed and implemented is achieving its intended results for participants. They are most valuable when contexts are straightforward and programs are linear in design: inputs leading to outputs that are managed to produce outcomes. But it also seems to me that RCTs often are oversold and overvalued when they are advertised as the "gold standard" of program evaluations, when they are put forward as the only valid way to establish the "truth" about programs' effectiveness. I have already emphasized that because of their positivist nature RCTs inevitably oversimplify programs and how they work, which can lead them to sidestep important issues like matters of emergence (such as the need to refresh staff training or take measures to reduce staff turnover during the evaluation) and the role of context (which can actually affect program participants while not affecting members of the counterfactual control group—for example, with changes in leadership in, or funding for, the organization that is operating the program). Thus they can (and not infrequently do) introduce *spuriously precise findings and hence an undue certainty among stakeholders regarding a program's inherent value or "true" effectiveness.*

Depending on what one wants to learn, other approaches to program evaluation must be considered and perhaps other epistemic frameworks adopted. Realist evaluations, using the repeated

---

[310] Ibid. p. 583.

collection of (for the most part) qualitative data to conduct case studies—both in one location and also in varying contexts—have their own ways of discovering and analyzing what's happening on the ground, including how programs are providing mechanisms that, in specific contexts, produce intended outcomes for their intended beneficiaries. Naturally, such evaluations too have their problems, the chief one being a notable lack of clarity and agreement on the definition of key terms. And there is the matter of plausibility: one does have to step outside a positivistic epistemology to accept and appreciate what realist evaluations can accomplish—which, at least in the United States, seems to me a remote possibility for many practitioners, evaluators, funders, policymakers, and academics.

In my view, it would be foolish not to recognize that in much of the modern world, positivism is the dominant research culture, at least for things like social programs. Consequently, in response to stakeholder expectations, RCTs are and will continue to be in high demand. Desired data will be quantitative, calculations of statistical probability will remain central, and they will continue to be cited as providing the required "proof" of a program's effectiveness. But we need not celebrate this fact uncritically.

Chapter XVI

WHAT CAN WE DO?

I owe it to any reader who has persevered this far to answer the question: "Can the ideas explored here be put to practical use in the social sector?" I think the answer is "Yes"!

Toward this end, I have a series of suggestions about how to help improve the design, implementation, and utilization of program evaluations:

1. Graduate schools offering degrees in evaluation should include courses on the history of science and on the epistemic underpinnings of various approaches to program evaluations.

2. The social sector needs an aggregated capital fund of some $100 million to be administered by an entity committed to financing high-quality program evaluations, but that also is agnostic regarding which evaluation methods are funded in each case. Specifically, RCTs should not be privileged over other means; the nature of the questions to be addressed should dictate the methods that are employed to answer them.

3. Furthermore, funded program evaluations should be required by funders *to pre-register with a commitment to publish their findings no matter what the results show*, as long as the proposed evaluation design meets

professional standards and proper evaluation practices were used. As a corollary, journals that report on program evaluations should require preregistration as a criterion to be met for an evaluation report to be published.

4. Evaluators who receive funding should be required by funders to make their raw data available to appropriate professionals to ensure high evaluation standards are met.[311]

5. All evaluations receiving funding should be required to state up-front the questions that the evaluation is supposed to answer, along with the outcomes it will investigate and the tools it will use to measure them.

6. While it may seem necessary in the course of a given evaluation to open new questions to answer and/ or new outcomes to assess, funders should require that such shifts should not be done without continued research on the original questions and outcomes—even where the results for the original study are not found to be important and only the revised research will yield findings of interest. It is important to remember that we also learn from evaluations of programs that fail to produce outcomes as intended.

7. Both those who perform and those who make use of evaluations need to be humble. No single evaluation of a program should be seen as providing dispositive information about its worth or what its future status should be. So-called "evidence-based" decisions need to be grounded in a full range of data that allow us to understand whether statistically clear results are

[311] Where this is opposed on the grounds of participant confidentiality, two measures should remove this obstacle: (1) ensuring that only professionals with the appropriate certifications (MD, APRN, LCSW, PHD, etc.) will review these data; and/ or (2) spending the time and resources necessary to de-identify the data.

sustained over time, and also on information that un-packs findings so that we can develop a reasonable un-derstanding of whom the program seems to help well, whom it doesn't, and through what mechanisms with-in what contexts it is working.

8.   Let's all of us resist getting seduced by the term "ev-idence." In every case, it is essential to know the ba-sis for the evidence being adduced about a program's effectiveness. In the words of the medical research-er George Lister, we should not "equate knowing or reciting the weight of evidence with comprehending the basis for that evidence."[312] In fact, I believe that the word "evidence" itself should constitute a red flag—one that should alert us to questions about the validity and reliability of the findings that are cited. Indeed, we should adopt a healthy skepticism re-garding evaluations that are proffered as "evidence" that a given program "works" or that specific practic-es are "best" practices—regardless of the prestige of the journal that has published them, the standing of the funders who commissioned them, and the pro-fessional reputation of the evaluator(s) making such claims.[313]

9.   It is always useful to remember that all evaluation methods, while informing us about some things, also blind us to others. For any given evaluation, we need to put in the time and work to get clear on these matters.

---

[312]   Lister, G. (2012). "2011 Joseph W. St Geme Jr Lecture: Five Things I'd Like to See Changed in American Pediatrics, Five Lessons I've Learned." *Pediatrics*; originally published online April 23, 2012; p. 963. available at http://pediatrics.aappublica-tions.org/content/early/2012/04/17/peds.2012-0146.

[313] To make the point more sharply: I don't believe that we will ever be in a posi-tion to identify a "best" practice for promoting desired outcomes in the social sec-tor. At best we can identify "good" practices, which we should expect to improve upon over time in light of accumulated experiences and new evaluative research.

In a way, this small book boils down to one big challenge: When picking an approach with which to evaluate a program, let's heed Weyl's caution and not choose one that will "nail on a roof by excluding the open sky."[314] And so I repeat what I stated in the Introduction, that *we must recognize how provisional any findings about program effectiveness must be; how modest we must be in asserting and communicating them; and how tentatively at best we should cling to them.*

---

[314] Weyl, H. (2009). Op. cit.

Chapter XVII

APPLIED EPISTEMOLOGY AND WHY I WROTE THIS BOOK

Back in Chapter IV, I introduced *instrumentalism* and *essentialism*—two fundamentally different understandings of what science should be about. During the last three decades of the 20th century (at least in the United States) the debate between instrumentalism and essentialism eventually gave birth to a period of intense "paradigm wars" among program evaluators. In heated and often less than civil exchanges instrumentalists, the *quantitative* evaluators who strove to explain things, disparaged what they considered the mush-brained essentialist *qualitative* evaluators whose goal was to understand things. These so-called "*quants*" insisted on an exclusively positivist view of science and thus of program evaluation, especially when the issue at hand was evaluating program results. "They demanded 'hard' data: statistics, equations, charts, and formulae."[315] (emphasis in original) When evaluating program impacts they insisted on the experimental research design of the natural sciences—that is, the use of RCTs. And so *their findings tend to assume a lapidary permanence in the realm of received knowledge about specific programs and their effectiveness—and even continue to be cited decades later.*

---

[315] Patton, M. Q. (2008). Op. cit. p. 420.

The quals, in contrast, while epistemically less clear than the quants, nevertheless derided them as simpletons who thought human realities can be captured through experiments in purely quantitative ways using independent and dependent variables. "The *qual's* world is complex, dynamic, interdependent, textured, nuanced, unpredictable"[316]—and not always directly accessible to our senses. Thus *quals* tend to use case study methods and go about their evaluations by collecting stories and more stories and even more stories (through interviews, focus groups, observations, video recordings, etc.). Consequently, *their findings emerge iteratively and are recognized as inherently and eternally incomplete.*

Today, at least according to public pronouncements by both *quals* and *quants*, the conflict has been resolved. The solution, as proffered for public consumption, is to embrace the need for both, for "mixed methods" as discussed in Chapter XIV. But as I mentioned in the Prologue, I perceive that below this mutual hugging, there is mischief afoot. What I regard as this false harmony thinly disguises the deeper issue of the competing yet incompatible world views of instrumentalism and essentialism. And as I see it, *instrumentalism—and particularly positivism its most rigid and even toxic form—has emerged dominant in our culture.* Consider the fact that already in middle schools (if not earlier) and all the way through institutions of higher learning, STEM[317] studies are growing rapidly while the humanities are being cut. "Shut up and calculate!" is alive and prospering while the arts, literature, history, and philosophy are being starved and driven into what is, at best, a marginal status. Yes, this is a generalization that no doubt has numerous and noteworthy exceptions, but as I see it they are the "exceptions that prove the rule."

---

[316] Ibid.

[317] Science, Technology, Engineering, and Mathematics.

So this oeuvre most definitely should be read as a determined attempt to slow down and moderate the positivist tide of history as I see it unfolding. The domination of technology in framing our economic, political, and educational spheres is overwhelming. Symptomatic is the development of Artificial Intelligence, which its creators know full well has incredibly dangerous potential. Nevertheless, AI is being supercharged without any serious investigation into the essential human (ethical) questions it poses. So too, even more alarmingly, CRISPR genome editing technology is spreading rapidly around the globe and being heralded for its potential to perform medical miracles. But there are few if any institutional checks and balances regarding its use. In fact, some scientists are working on gene editing outside any institutions and hence without any institutional constraints such as might be posed by institutional review boards. All this is rolling ahead even though alarms are being raised, including the potential for CRISPR technology to be weaponized and become readily available for militaries and terrorists. Indeed, CRISPR weapons might well become more deadly than nuclear weapons and destabilize the equilibrium of "mutual assured destruction" that so far has prevented nuclear wars.[318]

Limited as I am by my life experiences and the domains of my professional endeavors, I have chosen to communicate my existential anguish through a specific case where I can claim at least a modest level of competence: the epistemic interrogation of social program evaluations.

In my view, using positivist evaluation methods as a default ultimately is "scientistic"—but is not good science at all. Good science requires

---

[318] Werner, E. (2019). "The Coming CRISPR Wars: Or why genome editing can ecome more dangerous than nuclear weapons." ResearchGate. Oxford Advanced Research Foundation.

us to look for the kinds of evidence that will answer even our most basic questions: questions that we should frame as hypotheses that, in any given instance, might well need to be researched qualitatively rather than quantitatively; essentially rather than instrumentally; generatively rather than counterfactually; configurationally rather than successionally; and using case studies rather than experiments.[319]

But I don't want to be associated with calls for what some authors call an "inclusionist" approach or the need for simply "broader evidence" when evaluating social programs.[320] Arguing for treating any kind of evidence as valid or relevant no matter how or by whom it's been collected is exactly the kind of fuzzy-headed group hugging that undermines disciplined thought and reasoned exploration of the pros and cons, the strengths and weaknesses, of the various professional evaluation methods in use today; in particular, it ignores the epistemic assumptions and beliefs that underly them. So I have narrowed the range of evaluation methods I consider herein so that I might examine only a couple at some depth. In doing so I offer realist evaluations as a counter-point to RCTs not because I think they are superior to RCTs, but rather as a device for illustrating the cost of not "comprehending the basis for the evidence" produced by RCTs and to legitimize the appropriate use of alternative ways of understanding programs and their performance.

Fuzzy thinking serves nobody well and can do a great deal of harm. In the case of program evaluations, fuzzy thinking can lead policymakers and funders to insist on the use of RCT evaluations in instances where there is no rational reason to do so, or long before

---

[319] Greenhalgh T., Wong G., Jagosh J., Greenhalg, J., Manzano, A., Westhorp G. & Pawson, R. (2015). Op. cit.

[320] See, e.g. Schorr, E. B. (2020). "Broader Evidence for Bigger Impact." *Stanford Social Innovation Review*. Fall. pp. 50-55.

doing so can be justified.[321] It can lead us to believe that we know more than we really do (e.g., that a program "works" or "doesn't work") and thus lead us into rash decisions—for instance to decide either to discontinue or to grow or replicate a program based on the wrong kinds of data—or data that are much too simplistic by design, and incomplete by their nature. It can lead to troglodyte rejections of the utility of evaluations altogether (as in the brouhaha regarding the 21st Century Community Learning Centers described in Chapter XIV). It can lead to program nihilism, the belief that "really, nothing works" for helping this or that group—and thereby be used to legitimize political decisions to steer funding away from them; it can lead us to confuse explanation with understanding. It can lead us to ask misinformed questions, poorly conceived questions, or the wrong questions.

I would not have put all the time and effort into writing this book if I did not value program evaluations; indeed I am *convinced that evaluations, when used in an informed way are helping to better our world—but they also are being used in ways that damage it.* So in the end, despite my upset and pessimism about the state of our society and its culture, this opus is a small work of hope. A hope that it will prove useful to evaluators and practitioners—and also to funders and policymakers as well as other key stakeholders—who are passionate about the value to our society of effective social programs. Incontrovertibly, social programs are a fundamental part of our society's safety net, and as such are essential to narrowing the gap between the well-off and those who are marginalized, disempowered, or facing huge challenges and outright barriers (institutional, socioeconomic, physical, and/or psychological) along their life pathways.

---

[321] Julnes, G., Mark, M., & Shipman, S. (2022). Op. cit.

Knowledge, even though ephemeral, even though it is epistemically contextualized, is essential for us to act meaningfully; it is far better than no knowledge at all.

Or, in the wise observation of Sir Austin Bradford Hill, who pioneered the use of RCTs in medical research but also fought against a reductive reliance on them,

> All scientific work is incomplete—whether it be observational or experimental. All scientific work is liable to be upset or modified by advancing knowledge. That does not confer upon us a freedom to ignore the knowledge we already have, or to postpone the action that it appears to demand at a given time.[322, 323]

As I said in the Prologue, I have an unwavering conviction that *when done well and used well program evaluations have a lot to contribute to making the world a better place.* Without evaluations, we are unlikely to learn enough about how to design and provide effective programming reliably and sustainedly to the people among us who need them to live the kinds of lives to which they aspire—for themselves, for their children, for their families and friends and neighbors.

---

[322] Hill, A. B. (1965). "The environment and Disease: Association or Causation." *Proceedings of the Royal Society of Medicine; Section on Occupational Medicine. President's Address.*

[323] My thanks to Jonathan Borak for bringing Sir Austin to my attention.

Synopsis

KEY POINTS ON WHICH THE LOGIC
OF THIS BOOK RESTS

This Synopsis is intended to help orient those readers who by-passed the first two chapters. It also should serve all readers as a quick reference guide to the major issues that emerge in the course of this book, particularly as they are pertinent to the assumptions and beliefs that underlie evaluations of social programs. Some key points:

o *Ontology* is the study of the nature of reality. The two major approaches to this subject are (a) *idealism*, which posits that all perceptions and concepts of reality are ultimately creatures of the human mind and only tenuously related to what is "out there"; and (b) *materialism*, which insists that reality as we know it exists independently of human thought. While idealism (as first proposed by the ancient Greeks) has never been refuted fully, materialism has become the dominant perspective of contemporary American society in general and characterizes much of the scientific worldview.

o Of the various approaches to scientific materialism, *positivism* largely holds sway. Its adherents argue that the only relevant data for scientists to consider are those collected experimentally and that thinking about things that cannot be measured is not science—it is metaphysics or, in their view, "pseudoscience" at best. RCTs are best understood as the most fully realized positivist version of program evaluation.

o Epistemology is the study of knowledge, how we acquire it, and how we distinguish knowledge from mere beliefs. The two major epistemic approaches relevant to science are instrumentalism and essentialism.

• *Instrumentalism* sees science, its theories, and its calculations as a toolbox for making predictions about events that subsequently will emerge. The object of science is not to understand what the world is, nor to have theories about what exists, but is only to calculate and make predictions about what data new observations and measurements will find given a set of initial conditions. Thus RCT program evaluations, quintessentially instrumental, are designed to establish how effective programs are by predicting new data sets (specifically about outcomes) they will yield. The approach is designed to minimize as much as possible human subjectivity.

• In contrast, *essentialism* is focused on how to understand the world as organized through our culturally acquired methods of classification and the use of symbols to represent them. All culturally meaningful categories have two kinds of characteristics: (a) *essential* features that their members must have to be included in a given category, and (b) *accidental* features that they may or may not exhibit while belonging to it. Essentialist thinking requires that researchers look behind easily observable phenomena to the essences, the indispensable features that lie behind them.[324] For program evaluators intent on understanding a program beyond documenting its

---

[324] Becker, A. (2018). Op. cit. pp. 139-144.

activities and results, this means asking generative questions such as "Through what mechanisms does the program actually work?" or "How do the characteristics of the organization that is providing the program influence program outcomes?" and so on. As this suggests, essentialism fundamentally necessitates a qualitative approach to research. Thus it becomes central to the use of "mixed methods" in program evaluations; and specifically, to what are called "realist evaluations"—which, in this oeuvre, are counterposed to RCTs.

o The concept of causality, of linear cause and effect, is central to any attempt to evaluate program outcomes. Causality rests on the concept of time—or at least duration—in terms of which we make assessments of (a) given conditions, (b) actions to influence them, and (c) consequences. The problem here is that there is no general agreement among theoretical physicists on what, exactly, constitutes time—or even whether it exists at all. So the best we can do is use watches and related ways to measure duration—that is, what we arbitrarily decide to think of as time for our purposes. So time inherently is not a scientific concept; it is a metaphysical construct whose validity cannot be established. Consequently, cause and effect, too, have to be considered a metaphysical matter, not a scientific one. And since programs work within a linear cause-and-effect framework, evaluations of programs have to be seen—at least partly—as metaphysical rather than wholly scientific undertakings.

o Given the metaphysical aspect of all approaches to program evaluation, their findings can never be fundamentally "true"—nor "false" for that matter. At best, they can be stated in terms of probability. It follows, then, that there can be no "gold standard" that makes one approach to program evaluation inherently better than another. All that can be said is that different approaches to program evaluation ask and attempt to answer certain questions while ignoring other, equally important questions. Thus they produce different kinds of data for different kinds of purposes—and fail to produce what might be equally or even more important findings.

About the Author

Born in 1943 in New York City, I have spent much of my life as an outsider. My mother and father divorced when I was three and she remarried when I was six. Her new husband moved us from New York to Bern, Switzerland, where he studied medicine and I entered first grade in a rural three-room schoolhouse. After a short time, as my education progressed with the support of exceptional teachers, I became trilingual[325] and bicultural as well. And inevitably, in the course of the six years or so that we lived there, my personality developed through the filter of Swiss culture. But then we returned to America when I was twelve, and again I was an inept outsider, this time contending with American teenage culture and an antisemitism that was entirely new to me. It almost seems preordained that I would study anthropology, the quintessential outsider's social science, first at the University of Arizona and then in graduate school at Yale.

So fundamentally I think of myself as a male Swiss-American, a secular Jew, a serious thinker, and an incurable skeptic—with a wonderful wife and daughter and some great friends and admirable colleagues. Professionally, my identity is that of a former psychotherapist and an applied social scientist with an abiding commitment to work toward solutions to serious and persistent societal problems.

---

[325] High German, Bernese German, and English.

This explains why, after attaining tenure in Anthropology/Sociology at what now is Southern Connecticut State University in the 1960s, I found myself uncomfortable as an academic. So I resigned from that position (against the advice of almost everybody I knew) to return to graduate school for a degree in social work in order to find a job that had more immediate societal relevance, at least to me. With this degree in hand, I took a series of positions working with outsiders—marginalized and disenfranchised people suffering with severe mental illnesses and living in dire circumstances—first as a front-line clinician and then in management. (Concurrently I built up a private psychotherapy practice.)

Eventually, I was appointed to the position of Superintendent (CEO) of Connecticut's sole public acute care psychiatric hospital, and thus embarked on a six-year project leading the turn-around of a rather dysfunctional institution. This was a massive team effort with many extraordinary contributions by nurses, clinicians, physicians, and managers. I discuss this phase of my work in my book Working Hard—and Working WELL where I describe how we hit a lot of bumps in the road; but we succeeded, and ultimately received a rating of "Accreditation with Commendation" from the Joint Commission on Accreditation of Healthcare Organizations (JCAHO). This is the background against which I developed my ideas about data-supported and results-driven performance management. Naturally, I brought these experiences forward into my subsequent work.

Rather unexpectedly my friend Michael Bailin, then President of the Edna McConnell Clark Foundation (EMCF), offered me the position of Director of Assessment and Knowledge Development (Evaluation), which allowed me to deepen my knowledge of evaluation and the social sector in general. After the better part of a decade at EMCF I moved on to build a consulting practice focused on performance management in the delivery of social services (in both the public and nonprofit sectors), as well as on social investing (which at the time was a relatively new concept in the world of philanthropy) and the utilization of program evaluations. Over several decades I acted as a consultant to foundations and to nonprofit and public agencies in this country, in Northern Europe, and Israel. After I retired in my mid-seventies, quite unexpectedly I was given the opportunity to lead the design and implementation of a start-up social investment fund called the Connecticut Opportunity Project (CTOP), an initiative of Dalio Education. CTOP now invests in nonprofit organizations working to improve the lives and prospects of severely disengaged, marginalized young people. (I discuss this work a bit more in the Acknowledgements.)

For the last 46 years, I have had the great fortune to be married to my wife Elaine, a wonderful, smart, generous, nurturing woman, and a terrific mother and psychotherapist to boot. Elaine and I are the parents of Lisa, our beloved and much-admired daughter who is devoted to working in the nonprofit sector—which warms the cockles of her parents' hearts.

Along the way I spent a couple of decades studying both karate and judo until injuries wore me down; and starting at age 50, in response to Elaine's urging that I act on a long-expressed desire, I took up the study of classical guitar. But, due to the encroaching debilities of dotage, I recently had to give this up. And so I turned again to writing—and finally finishing—this book.

As of January of this year (2024), I have retired once again; this time, I hope and believe, permanently. But don't ask me what that means…

References

1. Abt Associates (2021). "Roca's Impact: An Update on External Evaluation Results." Accessible at: https://rocainc.org/wp-content/uploads/2021/09/Roca-Evaluation-Update%5EJ-September-2021.pdf).

2. Andersen, David. (2019). "Proven programs are the exception, not the rule." *Guest Post: The GiveWell Blog.* Accessible at: https://blog.givewell.org/2008/12/18/guest-post-proven-programs-are-the-exception-not-the-rule/.

3. Andrade, C. (2019). "The *P* Value and Statistical Significance: Misunderstandings, Explanations, Challenges, and Alternatives." *Indian Journal of Psychological Medicine.* Vol. 41(3).

4. Andrée Löfholm, C., Brännström L., Olsson M., & Hansson K. (2013). "Treatment-as-usual in effectiveness studies: What is it and does it matter?" *International Journal of Social Welfare.* Vol. 22:25–34.

5. Apel, K-O. The Erklären-Verstehen controversy in the philosophy of the natural and human sciences. In: Fløistad G. (Ed.). *La Philosophie Contemporaine/ Contemporary Philosophy.* International Institute of Philosophy / Institut International de Philosophie, vol 2. Springer. pp. 19-49.

6. Astbury, B. & Leeuw, F. L. (2010). "Unpacking Black Boxes: Mechanisms and Theory Building in Education." *American Journal of Evaluation* Vol. 31, pp. 363-381.

7. Audubon, J. J. (1840). *Birds of America From Drawings Made in the United States and Their Territories.* J. J. Audubon and B. Chevalier.

8. Barnes, C. E. (2022). "Prediction versus Accommodation." *Stamford Encyclopedia of Philosophy. Zalta,* E. N. Zalta & Nodelman, U. (eds.). Accessible at: https://plato.stanford.edu/archives/win2022/entries/prediction-accommodation/.

9. Becker, A. (2018). *What is Real?* John Murray.

10. Befani, B. (2012). "Models of Causality and Causal Inference." A working paper that contributed to Stern, E., Stame, M., Mayne, J., Forss, K., Davides, R. & Befani, B. (2012) *Broadening the Range of Designs and Methods for Impact Evaluations*. Working aper 38. Department for International Development.

11. Benjamin, C. (1966). "Ideas of Time in the History of Philosophy." In Fraser, J. T. (Ed.) (1966) *The Voices of Time*. George Braziller. pp. 3-30. p. 9.

12. Berger, P. L. & Luckman, T. (1967). *The Social Construction of Reality*. Doubleday Anchor.

13. Brinkerhoff, R. O. (2003). *The Success Case Method.* Berrett-Koehler.

14. Bhaskar, R. (1975). *A realist theory of science*. Harvester Press.

15. Boris, E. T. & Winkler, M. K. (2013). "The Emergence of Performance Measurement as a Complement to Evaluation Among U.S. Foundations." In Nielsen, S. B. & Hunter, D. E. K. (Eds.) (2013). Op.cit. pp. 69-80.

16. Bourdeau, M. (2023). "Auguste Comte." *The Stanford Encyclopedia of Philosophy. Zalta, E. N. & Nodelman, U. (eds.). Accessible at: https://plato.stanford.edu/archives/spr2023/entries/comte/*.

17. Bowie L. & Bronte-Tinkew, J. (2008). "Process Evaluations: A Guide for Out-of-School Time Practitioners." *Research to Results Brief*. Child Trends.

18. Brantley, P. (2011). "What it Takes: Building a Performance Management System to Support Students and Teachers." In Morino, M. (2011). *Leap of Reason: Managing to Outcomes in an Era of Scarcity.* Venture Philanthropy Partners. pp. 117-126.

19. Bridges, M. R. (2206). "Activating the Corrective Emotional Experience." *Journal of Clinical Psychology: In Session.* Vol. 62(5):551-568. Wiley.

20. Byng, R., Norman, I., Redfern, S. & Jones, R. (2008). "Exposing the key functions of a complex intervention for shared care in mental health: A case study of a process evaluation." *BMC Health Services Research*. Vol. 8:274.

21. Caroll, S. (2019). *Something Deeply Hidden: Quantum Worlds and the Emergence of Spacetime.* Dutton.

22. Chakravartty, A. (2017). "Scientific Realism." The Stanford Encyclopedia of Philosophy (Summer Edition). Zalta, E. N. (ed.). Accessible at: https://plato.stanford.edu/archives/sum2017/entries/scientific-realism/.

23. Changeux, J.-P. & Ricoeur, P. (2000). What Makes us Think? Princeton University Press.

24. Chen, H.-T. (1990). *Theory-driven evaluations*. Sage.

25. Chen H.-T. & Rossi, P. H. (1981). "The multi-goal theory-driven approach to evaluation: A model linking basic and applied social science." In Freedman, H. and Soloman, M. (Eds.) *Evaluation Studies Review Annual.* Vol. 6. Sage. pp 38-54.

26. Coalition for Evidence-Based Policy. Accessible at: Coalition for Evidence-Based Policy | Tackling US Social Problems Through Evidence About "What Works" (evidencebasedpolicy.org).

27. Cochrane Library. Accessible at: https://www.cochranelibrary.com/.

28. Cornell University Evidence-Based Living blog. "Randomized, Controlled Designs: The "Gold Standard" for Knowing What Works". Accessible at: https://evidencebasedliving.human.cornell.edu/blog/randomized-controlled-designs-the-gold-standard-for-knowing-what-works-2/.

29. Craig, P. Dieppe, P., Macintyre, S., Michie, S., Nazareth, I. & Pettigrew, M. (2006). *Developing and evaluating complex interventions: new guidance.* Medical Research Council.

30. Creswell, J. W. & Clark, V. L. P. (2017). Designing and Conducting Mixed Methods Research. Sage.

31. Dampier, W. C. (1929). *A History of Science and its Relations with Philosophy and Religion.* Cambridge University Press.

32. Daston, L. & Galison, P. (2010). *Objectivity.* Zone.

33. Daubert v. Merril (1993). 509 U.S. 579.

34. De Filetti, B. (1977). *Theory of Probability Vols. I and 2.* Wiley.

35. De Pierris, G. & Friedman, M. (2018) "Kant and Hume on Causality", *The Stanford Encyclopedia of Philosophy* (Winter Edition). Zalta E. N. Edward(ed.). Accessible at: https://plato.stanford.edu/archives/win2018/entries/kant-hume-causality/.

36. De Vrieze, J. (2021) "Landmark Research Integrity Survey Finds Questionable Practices Are Surprisingly Common." *Scienceinsider. Science.* July. Accessible at: https://www.science.org/content/article/landmark-research-integrity-survey-finds-questionable-practices-are-surprisingly-common.

37. De Waal Malefijt, A. (1974). *Images of Man.* Alfred A. Knopf.

38. Dilthey, G. (1883). *Einleitung in die Geisteswissenschaften.* Dunker & Humblot.

39. Droysen, J. G. (1867). *Grundriss der Historik.* Veit.

40. Durkheim, E. (1938; orig. pub. 1895). The Rules of Sociological Method. The Free Press.

41. Durkheim, E. (1951; orig. pub. 1897). Suicide. A Study in Sociology. The Free Press.

42. Dushoff, J., Kain, M. P. & Bolker, B. M. (2019). "I Can See Clearly Now: Reinterpreting Statistical Significance". Methods in Ecology and Evolution. Vol. 10. January. pp. 756-759.

43. Dymnicki, A., Wandersman, A., Osher, D., Grigorescu, V., & Huang, L. (2014*). Willing, Able -> Ready: Basics and Policy Implications of Readiness as a Key Component for Implementation of Evidence-Based Interventions.* Office of the Assistant Secretary of Planning and Evaluation, Office of Human Services Policy, U.S. Department of Health and Human Services.

44. Droysen, J. G. (1867). *Grundriss der Historik.* Veit.

45. Einstein, A. (1905). "Über einen die Erzeugung und Verwandlung des Lichtes betreffenden heuristischen Gesichtspunkt" [On a Heuristic Viewpoint Concerning the Production and Transformation of Light]. *Annalen der Physik.* Vierte Folge 17:132–148. (in German). Johann Ambrosius Barth.

46. Einstein, A. (1916). "Die Grundlage der allgemeine Relativitäts-theorie" [The Basis of the General Theory of Relativity]. *Annalen der Physik*, Vol. 49(7), pp. 769–822. Separately printed Berlin: J. Springer.

47. Emery, N., Markosian, N., & Sullivan, N. (2020). "Time." *The Stanford Encyclopedia of Philosophy* (Winter Edition). Zalta, E. N. (ed.). Accessible at: https://plato.stanford.edu/archives/win2020/entries/time/.

48. Fanelli, D. (2011). "Negative Results are Disappearing from Most Disciplines and Countries." *Sociometrics.* Vol. 90(2). March. pp. 891-904.

49. Fine, K. (1994). "Essence and Modality: The Second Philosoph-ical Perspectives Lecture", *Philosophical Perspectives*, Vol. 8, pp. 1–16.

50. Fixsen, D. L., Naoom, S. F., Blase, K. A., Friedman, R. M. & Wallace, F. (2005). *Implementation Research: A Synthesis of the Literature.* University of South Florida.

51. Fornacon-Wood, I., Hitesh, M., Johnson-Hart, C., Faivre-Finn, C., O'Connor, J. P. B. & Price, G. J. (2022) . "Understanding the Differences Between Bayesian and Frequentist Statistics." International Journal of Radiation Oncology. Biology. Physics. Vol. 112, No. 5, pp. 1076–1082. Published by Elsevier Inc. Acces-sible at: https://doi.org/10.1016/j.ijrobp.2021.12.011.

52. Frankfurt, H. G. (1998). "The importance of what we care about." *The Importance of What We Care About.* Ch. 8. p. 80. Cambridge University Press.

53. Geertz, C. (1973). *The Interpretation of* Cultures. Basic Books.

54. Geertz, C. (1983). *Local Knowledge. Further Essays in Interpre-tive Anthropology*. Basic Books.

55. Glaser, B. G. & Strauss, A. L. (1967). *The Discovery of Grounded Theory: Strategies for Qualitative Research.* Aldine.

56. Goicolea, I., Coe, A.-B., Hurtig, A. K. & Sebastian, M. S. (2012). "Mechanisms for Achieving Adolescent-Friendly Services in Ecuador: a realist evaluation approach." *Glob Health Action*. Vol. 5:18748.

57. Greene, J. C. (2015). "The emergence of mixing methods in the field of evaluation." *Qualitative Health Research*. Vol. 25(6), pp. 746–750.

58. Greenhalg, T., Humphrey, C., Hughes J., MacFarlane F., Butler, C. & Pawson, R. (2009). "How Do You Modernize a Health Service? A Realist Evaluation of Whole-Scale Transformation in London." *The Milbank Quarterly*, Vol. 87, No. 2:391–416.

59. Greenhalgh T., Wong G., Jagosh J., Greenhalg, J., Manzano, A., Westhorp G. & Pawson, R. (2015). "Protocol—the RAMESES II study: developing guidance and reporting standards for realist evaluation." *BMJ Open*. 5:e008567.

60. Greenhalgh T., Greenhalg, J., Pawson R., Manzano, A., Wong G., Jagosh, J. & Westhorp, G. (2016). "Quality standards for realist evaluation. For evaluators and peer-reviewers." *The RAMESES II Project*. Accessible at: http://ramesesproject.org/media/RE_ Quality Standards for evaluators and peer reviewers.pdf.

61. Guba, E. G. & Lincoln, Y. S. (1989). *Effective Evaluation: Improving the Usefulness of Evaluation Results Through Responsive and Naturalistic Approaches.* Jossey-Bass.

62. Guba, E. G. & Lincoln, Y. S. (2005). "Paradigmatic Controversies, Contradictions, and Emerging Confluences." In Denzin, N. K. & Linkoln, Y. S. (eds.) The SAGE Handbook of Qualitative Research. (pp 191-215). SAGE. (2005).

63. Guyer, P. & Horstmann, R.-P. (2023). "Idealism", *The Stanford Encyclopedia of Philosophy* (Spring Edition). Edward N. Zalta & Uri Nodelman (eds.), URL = <https://plato.stanford.edu/archives/ spr2023/entries/idealism/>.

64. Hacohen, M. H. (2002). *Karl Popper: The Formative Years 1902-1945.* Cambridge University Press.

65. Hansson, S. O. (2021). "Science and Pseudo-Science." *The Stanford Encyclopedia of Philosophy.* (Fall Edition), Zalta, E. N. (ed.). Accessible at: https://plato.stanford.edu/archives/fall2021/entries/pseudo-science/.

66. Harris, A. (2010). "Six Steps to Successfully Scale Impact in the Nonprofit Sector." *The Evaluation Exchange*. Harvard Family Research Project, vol, XV(1) p. 4.

67. Harris, M. (1968). *The Rise of Anthropological Theory*. Thomas Y. Crowell.

68. Hedström, P. & Swedberg, R. (Eds.). (1998). *Social Mechanisms: An analytical approach to social theory*. Cambridge University Press.

69. Hepburn B. & Anderson H. (2023). "Scientific Method." *The Stanford Encyclopedia of Philosophy*. (Summer Edition). Accessible at: https://plato.stanford.edu/archives/sum2021/entries/scientific-method/.

70. Hitchcock, C. & Rédei, . "Reichenbach's Common Cause Principle", *The Stanford Encyclopedia of Philosophy* (Summer 2021 Edition). Zalta, E. N. (ed.). Accessible at: https://plato.stanford.edu/archives/sum2021/entries/physics-Rpcc/.

71. Hill, A. B. (1965). "The environment and Disease: Association or Causation." *Proceedings of the Royal Society of Medicine; Section on Occupational Medicine. President's Address.*

72. Höffding, H. (2005). *A History of Modern Philosophy.* Translated from the German by B. E. Meyer. Dover. Vol. 1. p. 541.

73. Holt, C., Fawcett, S., Francisco, V., Schultz, J., Berkowitz, B. & Wolff, T. (established 1994). "SWAT Analysis: Strengths, Weaknesses, Opportunities, and Threats." *The Community Toolbox.* Chapter 3, Section 14. Available at: https://ctb.ku.edu/en/table-of-contents/assessment/assessing-community-needs-and-resources/swot-analysis/main.

74. Hossain, F. & Wasserman, K. (2021). *Using Cognitive Behavioral Therapy to Address Trauma and Reduce Violence Among Baltimore's Young Men.* MDRC. July.

75. Hossenfelder, S. (2022). *Existential Physics: A Scientist's Guide to Life's Biggest Questions*. Atlantic Books.

76. Hunter, D. E. & Whitten, P. (1976). *The Study of Anthropology.* Harper & Row.

77. Hunter, D. E. K. (2006). "Daniel and the rhinoceros." *Evaluation and Program Planning.* Vol. 29, pp. 180-185.

78. Hunter, D. E. K. (2011). "Using a Theory-of-Change Approach to Helping Nonprofits Manage to Outcomes." In Morino, M. (2011). *Leap of Reason: Managing to Outcomes in an Era of Scarcity.* Venture Philanthropy Partners. p. 104.

79. Hunter, D. E. K. (2013). *Working Hard—and Working WELL.* Hunter Consulting, LLC.

80. Hunter, D. E. K. & Nielsen, S. B. (2013). "Performance Management and Evaluation: Exploring Complementarities." In Nielsen, S. B. & Hunter, D. E. K. (eds.) (2013). Op.cit. pp. 7-17.

81. Hunter, D., Berlin, G., Moore, K. & Kuraishi, M. (2017). "Statistical vs. Social Significance." Leap of Reason Ambassadors Community. Accessible at: https://www.leapambassadors.org/ambassador-insights/statistical-vs-social-significance/.

82. Iannacci, F. & Kraus, S. (2023). "Configurational Theory: A review." In S. Papagiannidis (Ed). *TheoryHub Book*. Accessible at: https://open.ncl.ac.uk.

83. Ioannidis, J. P. A. (2005). "Why Most Published Research Findings are False." *PloS Medicine.* 2(8)e124. pp. 0696-0701.

84. Institution of Education Sciences. (2013). *Common Guidelines for Education Research and Development.* U.S. Department of Education and the National Science Foundation.

85. Julnes, G., Mark, M., & Shipman, S. (2022). "Conditions to Consider in the Use of Randomized Experimental Designs in Evaluation." *Journal of MultiDisciplinary Evaluation*, Vol. *18*(42).

86. Kaplan, D. (2024). *Bayesian Statistics for the Social Sciences.* 2nd edition. Guilford Press. p. 6.

87. Lange, A. F. (1866), *Geschichte des Materialismus und Kritik seiner Bedeutung in der Gegenwart.* Iserlohn: J. Baedeker.

88. Lehrer, J. (2010). "The Truth Wears Off." *The New Yorker, December 13.* pp. 52-57.

89. Lemire, S., Kwako, A., Nielsen, S. B., Christie, C. A., Donaldson, S. I., & Leeuw, F. L. (2020). "What is this thing called a mechanism? Findings from a review of realist evaluations". In Schmitt, J. (Ed.). *Causal Mechanisms in Program Evaluation.* New Directions for Evaluation, Vol. 16, pp. 73–86.

90. Leplin, J. (2011). "Enlisting Popper in the Case for Scientific Realism." *Philosophia Scientiæ* [En ligne]:11.

91. Levitt, H. M. (2021). *Critical-Constructivist Grounded Theory Research.* The American Psychological Association.

92. Lister, G. (2012). "2011 Joseph W. St Geme Jr Lecture: Five Things I'd Like to See Changed in American Pediatrics, Five Lessons I've Learned." *Pediatrics*; originally published online April 23, 2012; available at http://pediatrics.aappublications.org/content/early/2012/04/17/peds.2012-0146.

93. Martin P, Tannenbaum C. (2017). "A realist evaluation of patients' decisions to deprescribe in the EMPOWER trial." *BMJ Open* . 7:e015959. doi:10.1136/bmjopen-2017-015959.

94. Mayne, J. (1999). *Addressing attribution through contribution analysis: Using performance measures sensibly.* Discussion paper. Office of the Auditor General of Canada.

95. Mayne, J (2019). "Assessing the relative importance of causal factors." *CDI Practice Paper 21*. Centre for Development Impact.

96. Miller, H. I. & Young, S. S. (2024). "The Validity of Much Published Scientific Research is Questionable (Part 1)." <u>American Council on Science and Health (acsh.org)</u> Accessible at: https://www.acsh.org/news/2024/02/20/validity-much-published-scientific-research-questionable-part-1-17449.

97. Miller, C., Bos, J. M., Porter, K. E., Tseng, F. M., & Abe, Y. (2005). *The Challenge of Repeating Success in a Changing World: Final Report on the Center for Employment Training Replication Sites.* MDRC:xi.

98. Moore, G. E. (1963). *Philosophical Papers*. George Allen & Unwin.

99. Moore, K. A. & Metz, A. (2008). "Random Assignment Evaluation Studies: A Guide for Out-of-School Time Program practitioners". Research-to-Results. *Part 5 in a Series on Practical Evaluation Methods*.

100. Morris, W. E. and Brown, C. R. (2023) "David Hume", *The Stanford Encyclopedia of Philosophy* (Winter Edition). Zalta, E. N. & Nodelman, U. (eds.). Accessible at: https://plato.stanford.edu/archives/win2023/entries/hume/.

101. McCambridge, J., Witton, J. & Elbourne, D. (2014). "Systematic review of the Hawthorne effect: New Concepts are needed to study research participation effects. Journal of Clinical Epidemiology. Vol. 67(3):267-277.

102. Neyman J. & Pearson, E. S. (1933). "On the Problem of the Most Efficient Tests of Statistical Hypotheses". *Transactions of the Royal Society of London. Series A, Containing Papers of a Mathematical or Physical Character* 231 IX. pp. 289–337.

103. Nielsen, S. B. & Hunter, D. E. K. (Eds.) (2013). *Performance Management and Evaluation.* New Directions in Evaluation. Vol. 137, Spring.

104. Nielsen, S. B. & Hunter, D. E. K. (2013). Challenges to and Forms of Complementarity Between Performance Management and Evaluation." In Nielsen, S. B. & Hunter, D. E. K. (Eds.) (2013), pp. 115-123.

105. Nielsen S. B., Lemire, S. & Tangsig, S. (2022). "Unpacking context in realist evaluations: Findings from a comprehensive review." *Evaluation* 28(1): 91–112.

106. Nielsen, S. B., Jaspers, S. O. & Lemire, S. (2023). "The curious case of the realist trial: Methodological oxymoron or unicorn?" *Evaluation.* Sage. DOI: 10.1177/13563890231200291. Accessible at: https://doi.org/10.1177/13563890231200291.

107. Nielsen, S. B. & Lemire, S. (n.d.). "Nothing as Practical as an Analytical Strategy in Realist Evaluation: Findings and Recommendations From a Comprehensive Review."

108. Noorden, R. v. (2023). "How Many Clinical Trials Can't be Trusted?" *Nature.* Vol. 619. 20 July. pp. 454-458.

109. Olds D. L. & Kitzman H. (1993) "Review of research on home visiting for pregnant women and parents of young children." The Future of Children. Vol. 3. pp. 53–92.

110. Olds D. L., Henderson C. R. Jr & Kitzman H. (1994). "Does prenatal and infancy nurse home visitation have enduring effects on qualities of parental caregiving and child health at 25 to 50 months of life?" *Pediatrics.* Vol. 93. pp. 89–98.

111. Palenberg, M. A. (2023). "Causal Claims in Contribution Analysis." *Canadian Journal of Program Evaluation.* Vol. 37.3 (special issue):389-402.

112. Patton, M. Q. (2008). *Utilization-Focused Evaluation* (4th edition). Sage.

113. Pawson, R. (2002). "Evidence-Based policy: The Promise of 'Realist Synthesis'." *Evaluation.* Vol 8(3):157-181. p. 165.

114. Pawson, R. & Tilley, N. (1997). *Realistic Evaluation.* Sage.

115. Pawson, R. & Tilley, N. (2005). "Realistic Evaluation" in Mathison, S. (Ed.), *Encyclopedia of Evaluation.* Sage. pp. 362-367.

116. Perrin, B., Speer, S., Saunders, M., Stame, N., Stern, E. & Ofrir, Z. (2007). *EES Statement: The importance of a methodologically diverse approach to impact evaluation—specifically with respect to development aid and development interventions.* European Evaluation Society.

117. Plato. (375 B.C.E./2006). (Allen, R. E. translator and editor) *The Republic.* Yale University Press.

118. Popper, K. (1963). *Conjectures and Refutations: The Growth of Scientific Knowledge.* Routledge and Kegan Paul.

119. Popper, K. (1972). *Objective Knowledge.* Clarendon Press.

120. Prochaska, J. O. and Velicer, W. F. (1997). "The transtheoretical model of health behavior change. *American Journal of Health Promotion.* Sep-Oct. 12(1):38-48.

121. Public Library of Science. (2007). "Is Most Published Research Really False?." *ScienceDaily.* 27 February. Accessible at: www.sciencedaily.com/releases/2007/02/070227105745.htm.

122. Ritchie, S. (2020). *Science Fictions: How FRAUD, BIAS, NEGLIGENCE and HYPE Undermine the Search for Truth.* Metropolitan Books.

123. Rosenthal, R. & Jacobson, L. (1968). *Pygmalion in the Classroom.* Holt, Rinehart and Winston.

124. Ross, J. (2008). *Thought and World: The Hidden Necessities.* University of Notre Dame Press.

125. Savitz, D. A., Wise, L. A., Bond, J. C., Hatch, E. E., Ncube, C. N., Wesselink, A. K., Willis, M. D., Yland, J. L. & Rothman, K. J. (2024). "Responding to Reviewers and Editors About Statistical Significance Testing" *Annals of Internal Medicine.* American College of Physicians.

126. Shannon, D., Walsch, J. & Lennon, T. M. (2018). "Continental Rationalism." *The Stanford Encyclopedia of Philosophy* (Winter Edition). Zalta, E. N. (ed.). Accessible at: https://plato.stanford.edu/archives/win2018/entries/continental-rationalism/.

127. Shaw, J., Gray, C. S., Baker, G. R., Denis, J.-L., Breton, M., Gutberg, J. Embuldeniya, G., Carswell, P., Dunham, A., McKillop, A., Kenealy, T., Sheridan, M., & Wodchis, W. (2018). "Mechanisms, contexts and points of contention: operationalizing realist informed research for complex health interventions. BMC Medical Research Methodology 18:178.

128. Schiller, F. (2015). [1795]. *Letters on the Aesthetical Education of Man.* Grindel Press.

129. Scriven, M. (1972). "Pros and Cons about Goal-Free Evaluation." *Evaluation Comment: The Journal of Educational Evaluation. Vol.* 3(4), pp. 1-7.

130. Scriven, M. (1982). *Logic of Evaluation.* EdgePress.

131. Scriven, M (1987). *Theory and Practice of Evaluation.* EdgePress.

132. Scriven, M. (2005). "Causation." In Mathison, S. (ed.) *Encyclopedia of Evaluation.* Sage. pp. 43-47.

133. Searle, J. R. (2010). *Making the Social World: The Structure of Human Civilization.* Oxford University Press.

134. Silverman, A. (2022). "Plato's Middle Period Metaphysics and Epistemology." *The Stanford Encyclopedia of Philosophy* (Fall Edition). Zalta, E. N. & Nodelman,, U. (eds.). Accessible at: https://plato.stanford.edu/archives/fall2022/entries/plato-metaphysics/.

135. Simon, P. (1951). Originally published in 1796. *A Philosophical Essay on Probabilities.* Dover Publications.

136. Schorr, E. B. (2020). "Broader Evidence for Bigger Impact." *Stanford Social Innovation Review*. Fall. pp. 50-55.

137. Social Programs That Work. See: Evidence Based Programs— Social Programs That Work Social Programs That Work.

138. Spinoza, B. d. (1670). Theological-Political Treatise. Israel, J. (editor) Cambridge University Press.

139. Stang, N. F. (2023). "Kant's Transcendental Idealism." *The Stanford Encyclopedia of Philosophy* (Winter 2023 Edition), Zalta, E. N. & Nodelman, U. (eds.), https://plato.stanford.edu/archives/win2023/entries/kant-transcendental-idealism/.

140. Stern, E., Stame, M., Mayne, J., Forss, K., Davides, R. & Befani, B. (2012). *Broadening the Range of Designs and Methods for Impact Evaluations*. Working Paper 38. Department for International Development.

141. Sundell, K., Ferrer-Wreder, L. & Fraser, M. (2013). "Going Global: A Model for Evaluating Empirically Supported Family-Based Interventions in New Contexts." *Evaluation and the Health Professions.* Vol. 37(2). Sage.

142. The Federal Judicial Center & the National Research Council. (2011). *Reference Manual on Scientific Evidence.* 3rd Edition. The National Academies Press.

143. Thornton, S. (2023). "Karl Popper", *The Stanford Encyclopedia of Philosophy.* (Winter Edition), Zalta, E. N. & Nodelman, U. (eds.). Accessible at: https://plato.stanford.edu/archives/win2023/entries/popper/.

144. Ton, G., Mayne, J., Delahais, T., Morell, J., Befani, B., Apgar, M. & O'Flynn, P. (2019). "Contribution analysis and estimating the size of effects: Can we reconcile the possible with the impossible?" *CDI Practice Paper 20.* Centre for Development Impact.

145. Turn90. Accessible at: https://turnninety.com/our-approach/.

146. Weber, M. (2002) [1905]. *The Protestant Ethic and The Spirit of Capitalism*, translated by S. Kalberg. Roxbury.

147. Werner, E. (2019). "The Coming CRISPR Wars: Or why genome editing can become more dangerous than nuclear weapons." *ResearchGate.* Oxford Advanced Research Foundation.

148. Weiss, C. H. (1972). *Evaluation.* Prentice Hall.

149. Weyl, H. (2009). *Mind and Nature.* Princeton University Press.

150. What Works Clearinghouse. Accessible at: https://ies.ed.gov/ncee/wwc/.

151. Whitehead, A. N. (1933). *Adventures of Ideas.* Simon & Schuster; 1967 edition, The Free Press.

Bibliography

Articles and Book Chapters on Strategic Performance Management, Social Investing, and Evaluation

1. Hunter, D., Berlin, G., Moore, K. & Kuraishi, M. (2017). "Statistical vs. Social Significance." Leap of Reason Ambassadors Community. https://www.leapambassadors.org/ambassador-insights/statistical-vs-social-significance/.

2. Hunter, D. E. K. (2014). "Evaluating Organizational Impact and Outcome Measurement." In Hansen-Turton, T. and Torres ND. (eds.), *Social Innovation and Impact in Nonprofit Leadership*, New York: Springer Publishing Company.

3. _____. (2013). "Using a Theory-of-Change Approach to Helping Nonprofits Manage to Outcomes." In Morino, M. *Leap of Reason: Managing to Outcomes in an Era of Scarcity*, Washington, DC: Venture Philanthropy Partners.

4. Bohni Nielsen, S. and Hunter, D. E. K. (Eds. (2013). *Special Issue: Performance Management and Evaluation, New Directions in Evaluation.* Issue 137.

5. _____ and Bohni Nielsen, S. (2013). "Performance Management and Evaluation: Exploring Complementarities." In Bohni Nielsen, S. and Hunter, D. E. K. (Eds.). (2013). *Special Issue: Performance Management and Evaluation, New Directions in Evaluation.* Issue 137, pp. 7-17.

6. Bohni Nielsen, S. and Hunter D. E. K. (2013). "Challenges to and Forms of Complementarity Between Performance Management and Evaluation." In Bohni Nielsen, S. and Hunter, D. E. K (Eds.). (2013). *Special Issue: Performance Management and Evaluation, New Directions in Evaluation*, Issue 137, pp. 115-123.

7. _____. (2013). "Getting Out from Between a Rock and a Hard Place." *Stanford Social Innovation Review.* March 19: http://ssir.org/articles/entry/getting_out_from_between_a_rock_and_a_hard_place.

8. _____. 2013). "Steps to Successful Performance Management," *Stanford Social Innovation Review*. March 19: http://ssir.org/articles/entry/steps_to_successful_performance_management.

9. _____. (2012). "Tactical and Strategic Performance Management in Social Services." Published in Danish in *SOCIALIT NYT Magasinet om digital kommunikation i den sociale sector,* issue 14.

10. _____. (2011). "Using a Theory-of-Change Approach in Helping Nonprofits Manage to Outcomes." Published in Morino, M. *Leap of Reason: Managing to Outcomes in an Era of Scarcity.* Venture Philanthropy Partners.

11. _____. (2010). "A Means to Assess Social Investment Risk—and a Plea on Behalf of the People Who Need Nonprofit Organizations to Deliver the Value they Promise." *Philadelphia Social Innovations Journal.* 3: Spring.

12. _____ (2009). "The End of Charity: How to Fix the Nonprofit Sector through Effective Social Investing." *Philadelphia Social Innovations Journal*, 1: Fall.

13. _____ (2009). "An American's Thoughts on Managing Public Services in Denmark." Published in Danish as chapter 12 in Ejler N, Seiding H. R., Bojsen D.S., Bohni Nielsen S., and Ludvigsen F. (Eds.), *Nar Maling Giver Mening: Resultatbeseret styring og dansk velfaerdspolitik I forvandling.* Copenhagen, Denmark: Jurist of Okonomforbundets.

14. _____ and Butz, S. (2009) *Guide to Effective Social Investing.* Baltimore, MD and Washington, DC: Social Solutions, Inc. and the Alliance for Effective Social Investing.

15. _____ and Butz, S. (2009). *Yes We Can! Performance Management in Nonprofit Human Services.* Baltimore, MD: Social Solutions.

16. _____ (2006). "Daniel and the Rhinoceros." *Evaluation and Program Planning.* 29(2):180-185.

17. _____ (2006). "Using a Theory of Change approach to Build Organizational Strength, Capacity and Sustainability with Not-for-Profit Organizations in the Human Services Sector." *Evaluation and Program Planning.* 29(2):193-200.

18. _____ and Koopmans, M. (2006). "Calculating Program Capacity Using the Concept of Active Service Slot." *Evaluation and Program Planning.* 29(2):186-192.

19. Cassidy, EF, Leviton, LC., & Hunter, D. E. K. (2006). "The Relationship of Program and Organizational Capacity to Program Sustainability: What Helps Programs Survive?" *Evaluation and Program Planning.* 29(2): 149-152.

20. Coleman, R. L., Hunter, D. E. K., Vartelas, H. and Higgins, M. F. (1996). "Quality Management in Mental Health. II. Managing Risk of Dangerousness." *American Journal of Medical Quality.* 11(4):227-235.

21. Coleman, R. L. and Hunter, D. E.K. (1995). "Contemporary Quality Management in Mental Health." *American Journal of Medical Quality.* 10(3):120-126.

22. Hunter, D.E.K., Buick, W. P., Wellington, T. and Dzerovych, G. (1993). "Reorganization of a Hospitalization Service for Patients in a Community Mental Health Center: An Initial Evaluation." *Hospital and Community Psychiatry.* 44(3):271-275.

A Book and an Edited Journal Issue about Evaluation and Performance Management

1. Hunter, D. E. K. (2013). *Working Hard—and Working WELL.* Hunter Consulting, LLC; translated into Italian as *Working Hard Working Well: Guida Practica Al Performance Management.* Fondazione Lang Italia.

2. Nielsen, S. B. & Hunter, D. E. K. (Eds.) (2013). *Performance Management and Evaluation.* New Directions in Evaluation. 137, Spring.

Books About the Social Sciences

1. Hair, E. C., Moore, K. A., Hunter, D. E. K. and Williams J. (Eds.), (2002*). The Edna McConnell Clark Foundation Youth Development Outcomes Compendium.* The Edna McConnell Clark Foundation and Child Trends.

2. Hunter, D. E. K. and Whitten, P. (Eds.). (1993). *Anthropology: Contemporary Perspectives,* Boston: Little, Brown, 1975, 1979, 1982, 1985, 1987, 1990. New York: HarperCollins., 1993.

3. Tishler, H. L., Whitten, P. and Hunter, D. E. K. (1983, 1986). *Introduction to Sociology.* New York: Holt, Rinehart and Winston.

4. Nickles, M. N., Hunter, D. E. K. and Whitten P. (1978) *The Study of Physical Anthropology and Archaeology,* New York: Harper and Row.

5. Hunter, D. E. K. and Whitten, P. (Eds.) (1978). *Readings in Physical Anthropology and Archaeology,* New York: Harper and Row.

6. Hunter, D. E. K. and Whitten, P. (1977). *The Study of Cultural Anthropology,* New York: Harper and Row.

7. Hunter, D. E. K. and Whitten, P. (1976). *The Study of Anthropology.* New York: Harper and Row.

8. Hunter, D. E. K. and Whitten, P. (Eds.). (1976). *Encyclopedia of Anthropology,* New York: Harper and Row; Translated into Spanish as *Enciclopedia de Antrolopologia,* Barcelona, Spain: Ediciones Bellaterra, 1981.

9. Hunter, D. E. K. and Foley, M. B. Foley. (1976). *Doing Anthropology: A Student-Centered Approach to Cultural Anthropology.* New York: Harper and Row.

Clinical Articles and Book Chapters

1. Hunter, D. E. K. and Simpson, L. (1992). "Countertransference and Clinical Choices in Public-Sector Treatment of a Patient and Her Family." *Hospital and Community Psychiatry.* 43(9):924-927.

2. Hunter, D. E. K., Ferholt, J.B., & Hoffnung, R.J. (1991). "Back to the Future: In Search of Psychodynamic Family Therapy in the Treatment of Families of Individuals with Prolonged Mental Illness." *Family Psychotherapy.* 2:81-96.

3. Klein, R. H., Brown, S. L. & Hunter, D.E.K. (1990). "The Treatment of Severely Disturbed Patients in Long-Term Inpatient Group Psychotherapy." In Roth, B. E., Stone, W. N. and Kibel, H.D. (Eds.). *Dimensions of Group Psychotherapy with Borderline and Narcissistic Disorders*, Madison, CT: International Universities Press.

4. Hunter, D. E. K., Ferholt, J. B. & Hoffnung, R.J. (1988). "Family Therapy in Trouble: Psychoeducation as Solution and as Problem." *Family Process.* 27:327-338.

5. Ferholt, J. B., Hoffnung, R. J., Hunter, D. E. K. & Leventhal, J. M. (1986). "Clinical Investigators Under Stress: A Critique of Garmezy's Commentary." *Journal of the American Academy of Child Psychiatry.* 25:724-729.

6. Klein, R. H., Hunter, D. E.K . & Brown, S. L. (1986). "Long-Term Inpatient Group Psychotherapy: The Ward Group." *International Journal of Group Psychotherapy.* 36:361-380.

7. Ferholt, J. B., Rotnem, D .L., Genel, M., Leonard, M., Carey, M. & Hunter, D. E. K . (1985). "A Psychodynamic Study of Psychosomatic Dwarfism. A Syndrome of Depression, Personality Disorder, and Impaired Growth." *Journal of the American Academy of Child Psychiatry.* 24:49-57.

8. Hunter, D. E. K. (1985). "On the Boundary: Family Therapy in a Long-Term Inpatient Setting." *Family Process.* 24:339-348.

9. Hunter, D. E. K. (1985). **"**Biological Reductionism, Reductionist Behaviorism, and the Social Economy of Clinical Practice." *Family Process,* 24:352-355.

Acknowledgments

I want to start by acknowledging the generosity and support extended to me by **Barbara Dalio**. She, along with **Andrew Ferguson**, co-founded Dalio Education and The Connecticut Opportunity Project (CTOP), its social investment fund. As a result of a series of conversations with various experts in the fields of education and youth development, they contacted me to solicit my perspective on what they had been doing to date. Although I told them I was retired, I said I'd be happy to chat with them. And the meeting led, quite unexpectedly, to them recruiting me to help design and then direct CTOP. This social investment fund has the mission of finding, investing in, and supporting youth-serving organizations in Connecticut—more specifically, organizations that are helping to improve the lives and prospects of young people who have become disconnected from school and from work. The present oeuvre, elaborating on my longstanding involvement with and thinking about evaluation, was partly stimulated and written during the time that I was thus engaged.

It is essential that I also acknowledge my professional colleagues at CTOP—**Aimee Rincon, Adhlere Coffy, Amanda Olberg, Samantha Miller,** and **Andrew Ferguson**—for their enthusiastic engagement with me over a period of some three years as we worked together to develop, implement, and refine the CTOP strategy for social investing. More indirectly, **Barbara Dalio, Chris Lyddy, Rosa Ortiz,** and **Carolina Deakins** also supported this work. Information about CTOP is available at: https://www.ctopportunityproject.org/.

Michael Bailin, my close friend ever since graduate school, gave me a life-changing opportunity when he hired me away from the Connecticut Department of Mental Health and Addiction Services to join him as Director of Assessment and Knowledge Development at the Edna McConnell Clark Foundation (EMCF) where he had shortly before taken on the role of President. This launched me into the realm of the nonprofit sector with a focus on social investing and evaluation; and here I found a professional home where I have dwelt ever since. In this regard, it would be remiss of me not to acknowledge some mentors in the field of evaluation whom I met through EMCF including **Gordon Berlin, Kristin Moore, Patricia Patrizi, Michael Quinn Patton, Karen Walker**, and the late **Harold Richman**. In their own ways and with at times divergent views, they each helped me develop a perspective on evaluation and its practices and gain the confidence to look below the surface at some of the profession's tacit assumptions and beliefs. That's not to say by any means they would agree with all the interpretations and opinions I have presented here. And needless to say, whatever errors I have committed herein are entirely my own.

My friend **Mario Morino** deserves special appreciation. He was the architect and financial supporter of the Leap of Reason Ambassadors Community(access at: https://www.leapambassadors.org/), which is dedicated to improving performance in the social sector. He is also the author of the widely appreciated *Leap of Reasons: Managing to Outcomes in an Era of Scarcity*. Mario has valued and encouraged my work ever since I began developing my "theory of change" approach to nonprofit organizational consulting while at EMCF. Indeed, he generously financed the production and electronic publication of my previous book, *Working Hard—and Working WELL*, for which **Lowell Weiss**, assisted by **Cheryl Collins**, provided wonderful editing and technical support. Then, out of the blue, **Steve Butz**, at the time president of Social Solutions, Inc., footed the bill for a run of 5,000 hard copies. Many thanks, my friends.

Nicolaj Ejler, a Danish social policy and management researcher (now a private consultant in performance management), out of the blue reached out to me across the Atlantic via email while I still was working at EMCF. He said he had found me via internet searches on the topic of data-based, outcomes-driven performance management, that he'd identified me as a "thought leader" (a surprise to me), and consequently he asked whether he could bring a group of his colleagues from Rambøll Management to meet with me. For the ensuing visit Nicolaj brought **Steffen Bohni Nielsen** with him, who already was establishing himself as a leading Scandinavian program evaluator (and now is Director General of the Danish National Research Centre for the Working Environment). As a result of our ensuing discussion they invited me to Denmark to meet with their colleagues, which then led to some twenty years of my consulting with Danish public agencies in the social sector, nonprofit social service agencies, ministries, and foundations. Helping these organizations work through challenges they were facing enriched my understanding of evaluation and outcomes-driven performance management and ultimately led to my involvement with the Leap of Reason Ambassadors Community (and the publication of my book *Working Hard—and Working WELL.*

It would have been impossible for me to write this book if my good friend **Jim Phillips** had not invited me, some five years ago, to join a group of academic philosophers and mental health clinicians with strong interests in philosophy who have been meeting for decades studying the philosophical literature and its history, with occasional excursions into clinical matters. I have learned much more from this group than I have been able to contribute, and am very grateful to its participants—**Jim Phillips, Phil Stambovsky, Mel Woody, Ed Papa, Bob Kruger, Wayne Proudfoot,** and **Marshall Mandelkern** for the generosity of spirit with which they welcomed and have tolerated me ever since.

The following friends and colleagues were kind enough to read, comment on, and challenge statements I made in various drafts of this paper. They nudged, tugged and pushed me to improve it over many iterations. So: many thanks to **Gordon Berlin, Steffen Bohni Nielsen, Kristin Moore, Michael Quinn Paton, Jim Phillips, Jonathan Borak,** and **Chris Angermann**. And of these folks, a special thank you to **Gordon Berlin** and **Jonathan Borak** who patiently helped me to correct errors of fact and interpretation about aspects of RCTs and statistics, respectively. And the same thanks to **Jim Phillips** and **Mel Woody**, who did the same with regard to the historical and philosophical aspects of the book. It should be abundantly clear, however, that any remaining follies, bloopers, errors of omission and commission, and questionable interpretations are entirely of my doing; for which, of course, I am quite prepared to eat humble pie.

For his help in the diverse facets of bringing this book to market, I am indebted to my long-time friend **Chris Angermann**, President of Bardolf and Company, Publishers.

And of course my gratitude and deep appreciation belong to my treasured wife and eagle-eyed editor **Elaine Kertes Hunter** who has labored graciously through numerous drafts to identify and help clarify ambiguities and other infelicities in my writing—and to pick up typos as well.

Finally, my gratitude to the late **Patrick J. McCarthy**, professor of the humanities at the University of Arizona, who challenged me more than anybody to think clearly so I could write well…and vice-versa.

With apologies to John Dunne, no one is an island; we all are all part of the main.

Index

T

V

W